The Best of

men's file

Published in 2013 by Korero Books LLP,
32 Great Sutton Street, Clerkenwell,
London, EC1V 0NB, UK
www.korerobooks.co.uk
© Korero Books LLP, 2013
ISBN 978-1-907621-10-9
Printed in China

Men's File magazine is published by Matt Hind
Editor-in-Chief: Nick Clements
Art Director: Ryo Bamba and Dan Black
West Coast Editor: Gabe Sullivan
Tokyo Editor: Taka Okabe
www.mensfile.com

Photo: John Wagner

The Best of

men's file

Tracing the Roots of Style

Nick Clements

Contents

Tracing the Roots of Style

men's file: The First Four Issues

THE FIRST TIME I heard the term 'fanzine' was sometime in 1977, in *New Musical Express.* The subject of the piece was the hand-written and home-printed *Sniffin' Glue.* The brainchild of Mark Perry, this was the insider's view of subculture and, aimed at other subculture members, it acted as a medium through which style messages could be transmitted in the form of photography, graphics and language. It was always my intention that *Men's File* should be an elegant fanzine talking to a broad spread of older males who had been involved in style-based subcultures since the 1970s and had arrived today in a world that has been named by the consumer market as 'heritage'.

The original idea of *Men's File* was to be a one-off issue acting as a vehicle for my photography and the collections of clothing and objects I had gathered over the past 30 years (clothing, cars, bikes etc.). I wanted to involve participants from the underground revival scene and most of the individuals featured in the magazine are the stylists that move subcultures forward in terms of aesthetics in the widest sense. They are motorcycle or hot rod builders, leather workers, traveling artisans, clothing designers, fine tailors, painters, retailers and dedicated collectors. They come from a network I have built-up since my own involvement in the revival scene which started straight after punk and new wave – that burned bright and then died in just a few months. I know what you are thinking: "Can't these old farts do anything without mentioning punk?" I agree it's repetitive, but punk seems to have been be the watershed event separating, in historical terms, the home-made stuff and the slick, professional, consumerist stuff – and that's important to the existence of this magazine.

It was 2008 and I was doing a post-grad research degree in the Dept. of Fashion and Textiles at London's Royal College of Art with the working title: *The Influence of Revival and Re-enactment Subcultures on Contemporary Men's Fashion.* I needed to let the high-fashion obsessed academics know that there was a growing trend in heritage style that was rapidly being embraced by influential retail buyers and that it was mainly the hippest older types that were wearing it. Meanwhile the groundbreaking *DICE* magazine was making significant headway into the revival custom and chopper scene with reportage photography, humour and a "these are our friends" approach that had a lot of the energy found in the early home-made fanzines. Acting in paralell, the Canadian fashion journal *Inventory* came along and focused on heritage fashion and those that inhabited that world. This was about people making small batch, high quality clothing inspired by mid-century design and not about the revival scene, but they were all connected. *DICE* at one end and *Inventory* at the other. I thought *Men's File* could reach both those positions and simultaneously rope in perhaps another 10 or 20 sub-groups who used other types of mid-century clothing, transportation or music as a metaphor for style.

Men's File was my idea but I could never have done it alone. I was in the right place at the right time when I met those who would make the magazine happen. Nathan Small (now a successful photographer in his own right) cut his teeth on *Men's File* and not only shot amazing and imaginative stories but also did much of the photo-production. Photographer Matt Hind continues to do epic stories and has acted as an ambassador for us during his travels to the four corners of the earth. Our first art director, Ryo Bamba, designed and set a house-style on issues 01 and 02 straight from Central St. Martins school of art and whose dedication to work needs a special mention. Our second art director, Dan Black, remains at the helm of graphics and layout and brings his own personal look to the proceedings in issue 03 and 04. Photographer and writer (Curious) Gabe Sullivan from Laguna Beach has consistently brought us great images and stories from California and photographers Gary Margerum, John Wagner, Richard Okon, Teruyuki Yoshimura, Grant Ellis, Mark Choiniere, Vincent Prat and Neal Reed gave us the view from inside their individual realms. These people are the core of the first four issues, which form the basis of this book.

Nick Clements

architecturefile

ONE OF THE first things I remember noticing as a child exploring my local environment was that some buildings seemed to follow patterns of design that could be grouped into definite styles. My parents were well aware of the main schools of architecture and named them for me. In my home town Victorian villas were the norm so the prefabs near my primary school stood out as unusual and different. There were a few pre-war houses that mixed late art deco elements with international style aspirations and these actually created a feeling of mystery and excitement. To me, as a pre-high school boy, architecture offered a complete space in which design would actually guide or even predetermine the activities that happened within a building.

For some reason, and I still don't know why, it was those mysterious modernist structures that fired the imagination so much more than the austerity of the Victorian era, the perfect proportions of the Georgian or the feeling of impending doom offered by the neo-Gothic. Later I would start to make a mental note of any structure that appeared to be influenced by the modernist project, whether from the drawing-board of a disciple of Gropius or the far less predicable Lloyd-Wright. They then became points on a notional mind-map that represented an inhabitable territory. This is the land that I continue to live in as a photographer and re-enactor. *Men's File* was intended to showcase such landmarks as separate entities and as important components of larger photo-shoots. Other photographers widened the remit and brought in new ideas and an architectural theme was established.

Ruby's Diner,
Laguna Beach

46

At 30622 S. Pacific Coast Highway, Laguna Beach is a modernist building of significance. Modelled on a mid-century diner the structure appears to be a recent build although details such as the curved glass windows have the feeling of the original. The owners could not say if it was a recent construction or a restoration although anecdotally locals told us it is relatively new. A trip to the local planning office would have been enlightening but there was no time and we wanted to get these evocative images into the first issue of *Men's File* as an example of style in an everyday context – which is what we hope this magazine is all about.

Ruby's Diner is a chain of restaurants, mainly located in California, that has appropriated and restored original eating-houses and constructed new locations where the original could not be sourced. The food reflects the attention to detail in the buildings and serves really great burgers that taste fresh and meaty as well as all the other stuff you'd expect at a traditional diner but often with a modern touch. Check out the Ruby's Diner website to see examples of the period restorations Ruby's has undertaken. We suggest visiting a few while you're in Southern California.

www.rubys.com

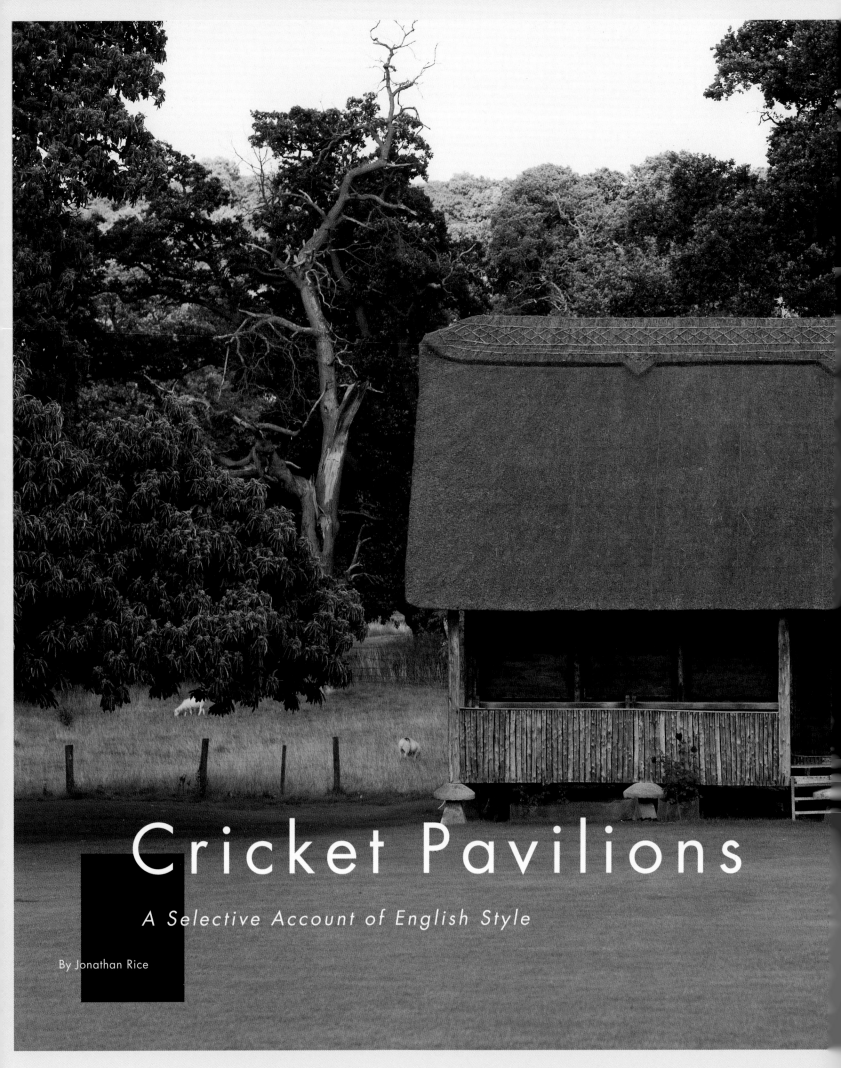

Cricket Pavilions

A Selective Account of English Style

By Jonathan Rice

Dotted all over Britain, usually at the edge of a well-mown field, are hundreds of simple but eccentric buildings which typify the English attitude to sport. They are cricket pavilions, each one an essential ingredient in a game in which the winning is truly not as important as the taking part. Every cricketer spends a huge part of his playing life inside a cricket pavilion, sometimes enjoying a full cricket tea of cream scones, egg sandwiches and something crunchy which might be a fruit cake; sometimes waiting to bat, padded up, nervously checking up on the opposition quick bowlers; more often cursing his luck for getting out to that wide half volley which was asking to be hit.

Some pavilions have Jacuzzis and massage rooms, but some make do with an outside tap and a dog-eared pack of plasters. Some have electronic scoreboards, a bar and slot machines, while others do not even have electricity. My favourites tend to feature half-empty trophy cabinets, and large honours boards with lists of chairmen, presidents and players of yesteryear. But even those with nothing more on the wall than a print of W G Grace in a broken frame, and an old tea towel which attempts to explain the Laws of Cricket, have a certain charm and tend to reflect the spirit of the club which has built its nest there.

Cheltenham College cricket pavilion, Gloucestershire. Built in 1865, W.G.Grace played here many times for Gloucestershire.

Chulmleigh village cricket pavilion, Devon. Built 1947, restored 2008

Bourneville recreation ground, Birmingham.

Bridgetown cricket club, Devon.

Bourneville cricket pavilion, Birmingham. Built in 1902 for Cadbury's factory teams.

Bourneville recreation ground, Birmingham.

Linton and Lynmouth cricket club, Valley of Rocks, Devon.

Chulmleigh village cricket club, new pavilion. Devon.

A good pavilion needs to be practical and it needs to be beautiful. Practical means it keeps the rain out most of the time, but beauty is in the eye of the beholder, so good pavilions come in all shapes and sizes. The word is derived from the Latin 'papilio' meaning a butterfly, and also (for reasons I do not fully understand) a rather grand tent. Originally, the players changed in tents, to protect their modesty, but nowadays players hope for a more permanent structure at the ground. Some are indeed permanent, well over one hundred years old in the case of Lord's, but others last less long. In 1993 I wrote a book on cricket pavilions, and of the fifty or so featured in that book, well over half have either been demolished or have been given major facelifts since then. Most of them needed it.

Architecturally there are no rules for cricket pavilions. They can be anything from Victorian Gothic piles to humble thatched cottages, they can be five storeys high or almost entirely underground. Some are in the urban heartlands of Britain, and some are found down the end of a long rutted track past barns, rusting tractors and fields of cabbages. Many are used for other purposes when there is no cricket being played: I know of at least three playgroups based in village cricket pavilions, two Rotary clubs and one pilates class. Another doubles as the village library and several are also war memorials.

Most of all, a village pavilion is a symbol of a simpler life we imagine can still be found in England's green and pleasant land, but is in reality long gone, and of a game that has always involved more sitting down than running around, and is all the better for it.

The British Prefab Photography: *Richard Okon*

It's surprising how many of (British Army) Major Peter Nissen's pressed-steel prefabricated structures still exist throughout Britain and the Commonwealth. This was perhaps the first universally accepted, prefabricated, multi-use, semi-cylindrical structure known as the Nissen Hut. Perhaps this ubiquitous object might still be an answer to our housing needs today if only it didn't remind us of army barracks, run-down farms and light industrial parks that have seen better days.

After the Festival of Britain in 1951 the public wanted to escape the past but still needed homes to replace those destroyed during the War and to accommodate the baby boom. Cheapness and speed are the two over-riding factors when housing is needed in a hurry and in post-war Britain the architect-designed prefab arrived just on cue. During the 1960s and 70s, as housing conditions improved and British working-class aspirations widened, the council-owned prefab carried a scent of stigma as it represented the temporary and evoked memories of wartime and homelessness. Today we can view such projects as case studies for modern design and applaud Mr Richard Okon for his single-minded and tenacious approach to portraiture and architectural representation.

www.richardokon.com

Photographer: *Matt Hind*
Production: *Point & Shoot*
Hair and make-up: *Lauren Gott*
Styling: *Warren Alfie Baker*
Model: *Jordan Hampton*, Next L.A.

THE JOSEPH EICHLER HOUSE

Joseph Eichler moved from New York to Los Angeles in the late 1940s. He lived in a 'Usonian'* dwelling designed by Frank Lloyd Wright which became the inspiration for Eichler Homes Inc. founded in 1949 to develop affordable modernist homes for post-war American families. Joseph Eichler is now recognised as the only developer in the United States to have produced modernist homes on a commercially large scale.

*An abbreviation of United States of North America used before the Second World War by Frank Lloyd Wright to denote a simple, affordable and distinctly American style of housing.

E-type Roadster 1973 XKE (V12).

121

Dining room table: Heywood Wakefield/M169G (1950 – 1955)
Chairs: Heywood Wakefield/M151A (1950)
Teapot set: Judith Weber (2006)
Buffet trolley: Salton Hotable (1960)
Yellow figurines: Hedi Schoop (circa 1950)
Vase: Bauer Pinnacle Vase (2000)
Stereo console: Telefunken (1963)

123

Jordan Hampton, Next Models L.A.

Eichler Inc. employed progressive architects such as Claude Oakland, Raphael Soriano, Austen and Allen, A. Quincy Jones and Frederick Emmons. Championing unorthodox techniques for tract housing Eichler Inc. would go on to Build 11,000 homes, mainly in the Bay area of Northern California. The home featured here is in the town of Orange, thirty miles south of Los Angeles and was built by Jones and Emmons. It can be found in one of only 5 Eichler developments in Southern California

SELECTED DEVELOPMENTS
The Highlands, San Mateo, California
Palo Alto, California
Fairhaven, Orange, California
Granada Hills, California
Thousand Oaks, California

THE ARCHITECTS
In December 1950, Joseph Eichler's Palo Alto development was featured in the influential magazine Architectural Forum and named "Subdivision of the Year". The same issue ran "Builder's House of the Year". The house was designed by A. Quincy Jones and a synergy was immediately acknowledged by Eichler who invited Jones to visit Palo Alto. The two men worked together until Eichler's death in 1974 but the professional relationship was augmented by the partnership between Jones and fellow architect Frederick Emmons. Apart from commissions for churches, libraries, commercial offices and university campuses it is reckoned that the designs of the Quincy A. Jones and Frederick Emmons partnership accounted for 5,000 of Eichler's forward looking, now iconic, California Houses.

IMPORTANT PROJECTS
Palm Springs Tennis Club.
Pueblo Gardens Housing Development. Tucson, Arizona for developer Del Webb.
1954 Emmons House, 661 Brook Tree, Pacific Palisades, California.
Eichler Steel House X-100, San Mateo, California.
Faculty Centre, University of Southern California, Santa Barbara.
Joseph Eichler Housing Development, Granada Hills, California.
Joseph Eichler Housing Development,

www.eichlernetwork.com

127

Mid-century house in town of Orange, California built in 1962 by developer Joseph Eichler. Architects: A.Quincy Jones & Claude Oakland.

129

autofile

CAR-BASED SUBCULTURES are universal and have developed in the postwar era as complex layers that overlap and intertwine, creating a patchwork effect that brought life to the first issues of *Men's File*. We wanted to somehow relate to our readers the multiplicity of meanings inherent in the presentation of any car of a special epoch – which, in the case of *Men's File*, is normally the mid-20th century.

We asked men and women, with knowledge of historical styles, to improvise scenes from history that related to the vehicle in question. *Men's File* photographed these interactions in an attempt to better describe and extend the style possibilities available to car culture members and those who admire them. The locations, people, clothing and even gestures are carefully thought out. Films are often the inspiration for these photo-shoots, in particular the films of the late 1970s and early 1980s that sought to replicate the 1940s, '50s and '60s such as Bogdanovich's *The Last Picture Show* (1971) or Bigelow and Montgomery's *The Loveless* (1982). A simulation of a simulation? Ask Jean Baudrillard.

18

Viva Las Vegas

Parked in the lot of the Orleans Hotel is an unusual car. Made from slightly oxidised steel the lower body of this automobile has the feeling of a Ford Model A while the upper part, consisting of roof and rear quarters is made to resemble a German military helmet of the First World War. This is George Barris on acid, (if he had made rat rods), this is Whacky Races for real, this is Viva Las Vegas. (Continued page 22)

Car Clubs at Viva Las Vegas

The American hot rod / rockabilly scene is quite different from the British, Swedish or German scenes but they all have a love of fine rods, carefully greased quiffs and cools bikes in common. The great thing about Viva is there's something for everyone. There's great music, there are lead-sleds, hot bikes, burlesque, rat rods, tattoos and Latino car clubs. Then there's the weirdness of the lower order of Vegas hotels (The Orleans and The Gold Coast) in which the event is held. Entire banquets of low quality comfort food are on offer adjacent to black jack tables mostly manned by bus loads of Chinese tourists for whom the gambling is just another American stop-off. Ultra

fat seniors ride electric carts around the slot machines carefully budgeting their pensions to last the entire month at the casino and bored housewives proposition any single looking young hep cat on the Viva trail if he happens to be sitting close enough. Like a scene from a Vegas – based remake of The Loveless you can actually live a movie for a few days – if you keep your mind open enough and don't take your wife.

There are also salons of vintage clothing dealers. Some of the best in America bring their wares and offer very rare pieces at very reasonable prices. There are even a few British vendors such as Johnson Shoes selling replica

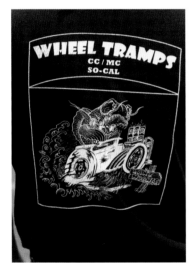

styles from the 40s, 50s and 60s. We sent photographer Nick Clements (a devotee of all things mid-century) to this gathering of the rockin' tribes to grab some photographs that might offer further enlightenment. The next VLV will be held April 1-4, 2010.

Links

www.vivalasvegas.net
www.orleanscasino.com
www.goldcoastcasino.com
www.johnsonshoes.com
www.barris.com

23

The Morgan Set

Photography: *Matt Hind*
Stylist: *Kenny Ho*
Hair and Make-up: *Nina Pach*

Let's call them The Morgan Set: perhaps a little decadent? Aesthetes who through outrageous self confidence took up Supermarine's finest and looked in the face of death time after time until their blood ran as cold as ice. Now the guns are silent all over Europe and the dust settled, a rendezvous takes place in high country style.

A London mews, rusty padlock opened, oil drained from sumps, plugs cleaned, points set and dried on two powerful J.A.P. (John Alfred Prestwich) engines. Telegrams sent and times and routes agreed; Norfolk bound.

A masked game of strip-rummy brakes thick ice and the blood warms. A siren, a beauty, femme fatale some say; but it was the War and everything was possible then when we all really lived. Like Mrs Gwenda Stewart who broke the hour record before the war in a Morgan three-wheeler strapped to screaming J.A.P. power at over 100mph.

Again they try to live but it's hard to get feeling back, at least those with no limbs have an excuse. Love is transient but style is always there. Now they will live only for the lines of the body and the speed. It's all they have left.

86

Morgan Sports Model (produced 1932 to 1939), powered by a J.A.P. V-twin and later a series of Matchless motors. This 1938 model is owned by Mr Simon Rayfield and powered by a Matchless MX4 engine now modified from 990cc to 1050cc. Miss Lizzy Tovell wears sunglasses by Cutler and Gross of Knightsbridge and Mr Simon Rayfield wears a leather Trailmaster jacket and gloves by Belstaff of Conduit Street.

(Left) 1930 Super Sports Aero, with J.A.P. engine. Currently owned by Mr Malcolm Barker.

(Right) Morgan Model F Super (produced 1938 to 1952). This particular 1949 model boasts a 10bhp Ford engine and was worked on at the factory by the founder's son, Peter Morgan. This car is owned by Mr Maurice and Mrs Eileen Cook (Centre background).

(Above) Miss Lizzy Tovell sits in 1938, Matchless powered Morgan Supersports and wears houndstooth scarf by Mr Richard James of Savile Row.

(Left) 1930 Super Sports Aero with J.A.P. engine (started production as the Aero and produced from 1920 to 1933). This example owned by Mr Tim Hodgekiss.

(Above right) Our brave boys, Wesley and Martin drive a 1955 MG TF owned by Mr. Geoff Hind. (Right) Mr. Gordon Bame wears shirt and tie by Timothey Everest.

94

1960 Ford Fairlane 500

Years of manufacture:

1955 – 1971

Named after Henry Ford's own Fair Lane estate at Dearborn, Michigan, the 1960 Fairlane 500 model came in two and four door options, the 500 being a variant from the regular Fairlane signifying superior trim and nothing more. Defined as a full-sized car of the era the Fairlane came in three engine sizes of 223 (straight six), 292 (V8) and 352 (V8-special) cubic inches with a maximum 300bhp at 4600rpm. The wheel base was 213.7 inches. Oh yes, the girl. It is our pleasure to introduce senorita Circe de la Rosa who is featured in two other stories in this issue of *Men's File*.

Photography: *Nick Clements*
Wardrobe: *Peter Gerber*
Hair and Make-up: *Robyn Nissen*
Production: *Gavin Schneider Productions*

Photography: *Matt Hind*
Wardrobe: *Peter Gerber*
Hair and Make-up: *Robyn Nissen*
Production: *Gavin Schneider Productions*

114

1934 FORD

Men's File would like to introduce our readers to this 1934 flathead V8 restored by Mr Les Boshoff. The young swimmer is Mr Kowie Theron and his date is the afore mentioned senorita Circe de la Rosa of Madrid, Spain.

Both Kowie and Circe enjoy dressing in finely tailored clothing that evokes the sometimes austere style of the 1930s and 40s. Kowie has a post graduate degree in modern languages and Circe is searching the world for adventure.

Mr Theron wears trousers by (RL) Rugby and belt by Ralph Lauren.

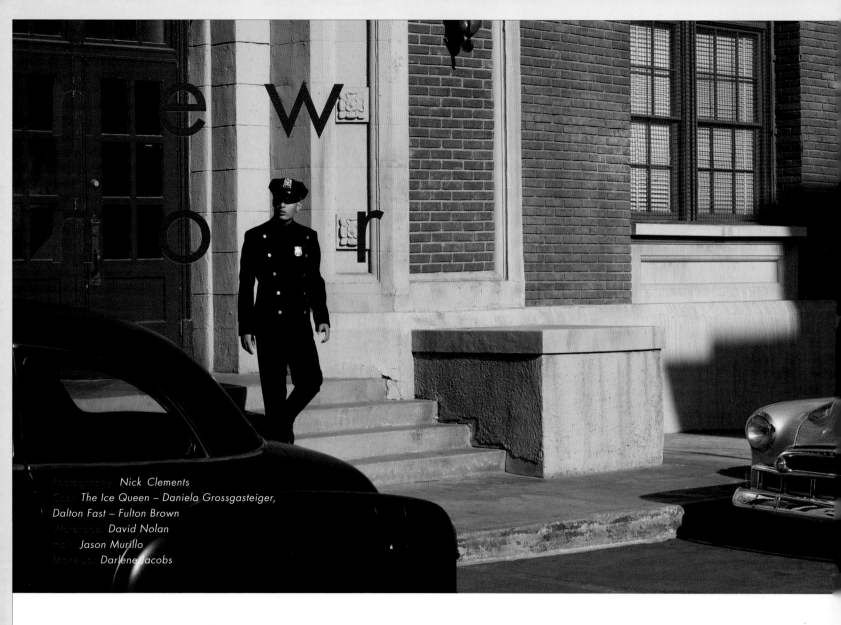

Photography: Nick Clements
Cast: The Ice Queen – Daniela Grossgasteiger,
Dalton Fast – Fulton Brown
Wardrobe: David Nolan
Hair: Jason Murillo
Makeup: Darlene Jacobs

A Day in Lead Sled City

Lead Sled City ain't one of F. Miller's. The Ice Queen didn't come down from an Austrian glacier in a fit of kindness, hoping to be forgiven for numerous sins of the mind too elaborate to air here. This is Gotham at it's most....

Aided and abetted by the excellent Mr Dalton Fast, the Alp-maiden from Bolzen stalks the streets of the city in search of fun and games of a most adult kind – robbery with violence that is. And what about 'love' you say? Beneath that icy exterior is pure liquid nitrogen at -100°c. She'll freeze your heart and break it into pieces with the same tool that did for old Leon down in Mexico.

When lead replaces gold and becomes the most valuable commodity, a new crime becomes common place: that of extreme beauty. In this world the ice blonde is found guilty of allure and escapes the long arm of the law on a pair of heels and with a .45 in her purse. In Lead Sled City a frozen water bullet in the head is the death of choice. I'll see you at Frank's place.

19

21

Royal Flush

Henry Gregor Felsen's Hot Rod Trilogy
by Simon McClean

Imagine my delight when I came across these three paperbacks in a secondhand bookshop in old London town. After just one read you are thrown into the world of souped-up gassers and ratted rods, danger and excitement, "shut down strangers and hot-rod angels", a real hormonal ride with disaffected youth.

First published in 1950, the novels tell the interlinked stories of Bud, Ricky and Link, their cars and their girls. A bunch of typical 1950s teenagers growing up in the fictional town of Avondale. Felsen originally wrote them as an adjunct to a contemporary road safety campaign and pitched each story as an instructive parable aimed at reckless road-going adolescents. There is a strong moral to the books: the struggle to do the right thing, peer pressure, and the expression of the individual. What the novels really convey though is the excitement, cool, and pure joy of riding in jalopies and racing on the open road, the complete opposite to Felsen's original intentions.

Reading such torrid pages conjures up a stream of flickering images, bending on chrome and distorted in wing mirrors, set to a soundtrack of Born-to-Run-Bruce-Springsteen's Nebraska, Street Racin'

blues. From the race in Rebel, Blacktop, Vanishing Point and Graffiti, Kerouac teen beat and Hud, the Last Picture Show small town America, even to the fifties fascination of Back to the Future. This is the universal myth, a bored, frustrated Luke Skywalker, racing his skyhopper on the far away planet Tattooine. The rites of passage of alienated thrill seeking youth in a post war, rock'n'roll, pre-Vietnam world.

The books should be on the American high school syllabus for these reasons. If Sophia Coppola had whispered 'Hot Rod' into her daddy's ear, instead of 'The Outsiders', by SE Hinton, they probably would be, and the landscape of 1980s teen movies would have looked very different.

Henry Gregor Felsen presents an early incarnation of the teen pulp novel, and through his clear love of speed and the fetish-like obsession in his detail on "hopped up rods" a particular evocation of a bygone era and a slice of teen life. They are Walt Whitman on wheels, an anthem to doomed youth, an ode to rodding, a ballad to the badlands, quite simply a love story to the automobile.

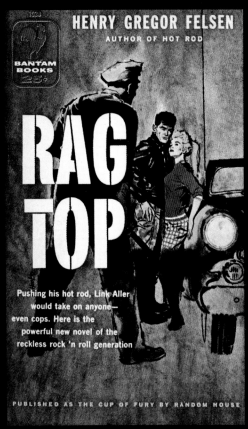

Brean Sands in a Bugatti

Photography: *Matt Hind*
Car: 1923 Type 13 'Brescia' Bugatti

Owner and driver of this robust Type 13 'Brescia' Bugatti is 32-year-old Ben Cox. Ben left school at 16 and trained as an aviation engineer. At the age of 28 he was chief engineer at Air Atlantique Group based out of Coventry and responsible for maintaining a substantial fleet of vintage aircraft ranging from vintage passenger biplanes to early British jet fighters such as the Gloster Meteor and De Havilland Venom. (continued page 112)

4 years ago Ben was responsible for getting a team together for a major overhaul of the R.A.F.'s Memorial Flight Avro Lancaster. A project he describes as hugely satisfying. Ben became a commercial pilot in 2010 and now divides his time between his responsibilities as an aerial survey pilot when the weather is fine and racing, trialling and hillclimbing his Type 13 Brescia when it is not.

In 2005 Ben bought a "tatty but airworthy" 1929 DH60G Gypsy Moth, the same type that Amy Johnson used for her record flight to Australia in 1930. With wings now finished, covered and painted Ben is now in the process of fitting a long-range fuel tank to increase the flying time and range to 8hrs and 650 miles! His next plan, embryonic at the moment, is to fly to Australia in it. When I asked why, he simply told me that a Gypsy Moth hasn't been down there since 1934. Seems fair enough. By the way, Ben is looking for a navigator. Any takers?

The Car

In 1921, Type 13 Bugattis placed 1st, 2nd, 3rd, and 4th at the Brescia Grand Prix. To capitalise on this success, Ettore Bugatti insisted that all subsequent cars with 16-valve, 4-cylinder engines would be referred to with the moniker 'Brescia'. Classic car racer Hamish Moffatt previously owned Ben's 'Brescia'. He bought her in 1952 for the princely sum of £12.10 shillings. Before the Second World War the car won The Brescia Cup, a Bugatti Owners' Club competition a total of 5 times. The car is still regularly put through its paces. Immediately after our shoot Ben prepped it for the 100-mile drive to Snowdonia, Wales and took part in The Vintage Sports Car Club's gruelling 2-day Presteigne trial.

www.prescott-hillclimb.com
www.alexanderboyd.com
www.bugatti-trust.co.uk
www.stetson-europe.com

116

motofile

FOR ALMOST TWENTY years the hip older man has sought to locate himself within motorcycle culture, whether rider, collector or connoisseur. The associations with freedom, style, the Counter Culture and subcultural style are painfully obvious but there's more here than first meets the eye.

Before we make any more assertions let's define our terms. I hope we can all agree that the Counter Culture is one of the manifestations of the ideology of the so-called left-liberal '68s who emerged out of the Paris spring, the civil rights movement and libertarian San Francisco. In 1968 they kicked down the walls of the establishment, offering a new wave of ideas and a replacement of the old structure. They demanded a voice for the young, believing that if everyone would embrace their belief system, the world would be a better place. Many confuse the Counter Culture with subculture or feel that they are more or less the same thing. They are not. Subcultural groups do not want rights, a voice or to be accepted or tolerated by wider society. Subcultures exist within society but do everything possible to absent themselves from conventional or pre-formed values. They don't want anyone else to be like them. Since '68 those behind the Counter Culture have gradually replaced the establishment and, through adopting certain strategies – such as appearing to offer the disenfranchised agency in their own destiny – have been instrumental in aiding the vast growth of consumerism and the commodification of all things.

Men's File's editorial has to find a balance between the Counter Culture/ consumerist position and the subcultural and collector's perspective. In the first four issues we covered the rebirth of the Brough Superior, the Ton-up day at Jack's Hill Café and the introduction of a new Royal Enfield retro-bike. This is the breadth of Men's File's remit.

Photography: Scott Pommier

TON-UP

It rained in England this summer. It rained for the annual Ton-up at Jack's Hill Café on the A5 at Towcester and nobody cared. Ancient British steel and polished alloy machines cut their way through M1 surface water like heroic homing eagles out of a 1940s sci-fi novel.

It wasn't only the bikes either. There was music from the Rocketeer DJ Sean Peschiera, a hep rockin' band called The Rapiers and the people and the rain and the bikes and the rain. It's called being alive daddio.

40

The Ton-up

43

The new Royal Enfield Bullet
Classic 500 (with vintage
N.Y. number plate).

THE NEW ROYAL ENFIELD

Bullet

Photography: *Nick Clements*
Wardrobe: *Kenny Ho*

Royal Enfield / Lewis Leathers
racing tabard.

Royal Enfield t-shirt.

1950s style racing sweater.

Let's not play around; the new Royal Enfield Bullet Classic 500 is not super-fast – but it is fun, very good-looking and the only new thing on two wheels that comes close to being anything like a traditional British machine. In continuous production since 1949 (the first model was introduced in 1932 but production ceased for WWII) and part of motorcycling history, the 2009 Bullet deserves attention and *Men's File* will be the first to introduce the three versions on offer to a series of styling possibilities presented by photographer and vintage collector Nick Clements.

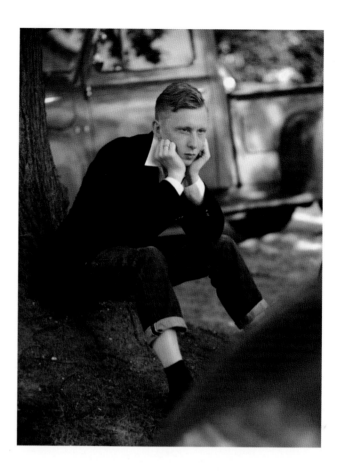

1950s style racing sweater (one-off) by the photographer.

As part of a long term investigation into the influence revival style has had on contemporary men's fashion; (represented in revival fashion tableaux) Clements has worked with Royal Enfield and two makers of British motorcycle wear, of unquestionable heritage, to produce modern apparel that takes the best from the era of earlier Bullet models active in Britain and the USA during the 1950s and 60s. Clements has plundered both the Californian desert-racing aesthetic and British café racer style to work with Lewis Leathers on a screen-printed racing tabard and re-styled Corsair jacket with white leather collar and cuff vents. This photographer takes great pains in the creation of his photographic tableaux and often adapts existing clothing

or makes replica garments from new, crafting a modern photographic image from a mix of historic and modern objects. Taking the Barbour International jacket – first used by the British International Six Day Trails Team in 1936, hence its name – Clements has replaced the map pocket and corduroy collar with green canvas salvaged from an unused 1942 gas-mask bag endorsing the vintage fabric with a lightly screened placement print featuring a Royal Enfield/Barbour ISDT combined logo (also designed by Clements). We've all heard of badge engineering on cars and motorcycles and it seems it works on motorcycle togs too. You change the trim and add a new logo and you have an even more desirable piece of clothing. Or maybe it's not as simple as that?

Clements is combining a myriad of factors here. Choosing three of the oldest brands in the world of motorcycling – Royal Enfield (powered bicycles from 1898), Lewis Leathers (outfitters from 1894 and motorcycle apparel from 1926) and Barbour (waterproof clothing from 1894) he is tapping into a first class heritage line. Both Barbour and Lewis Leathers still manufacture in the UK which adds a perceivable authenticity to the clothing Clements has created and fits in well to the photographs. Royal Enfield, on the other hand, is made in Chennai, India (since 1955) and used daily by thousands of Indians as a practical workhorse. For me at least (and I suspect most serious motorcyclists), this continued use of a bike, only slightly modified since the 1950s, through heat and dust for five decades puts the Bullet in an unassailable position in terms of authenticity.

80

Mr Nathan Small wears Lee 101 jeans
and Mr Billy Howard-Price wears vintage
jodhpurs by Huntsman of Savile Row.
Both wear t-shirts by Royal Enfield.

Ms Rebecca Horrox wears original (AMF period) Harley-Davidson jacket and Mr Billy Howard-Price wears 1940s replica Harley Davidson jacket by Real McCoy's.

(Above) The new Royal Enfield Bullet Classic 500 with vintage N.Y. number plate.

83

Royal Enfield / Lewis Leathers
Corsair jacket with white collar and cuff inserts.

The new Bullet EFI models are air cooled, fuel injected 500cc singles with a rounded pot and large fins giving the unit constructed power-plant old-skool looks and a traditional large British single feel when on the road. Trawling through the Royal Enfield back catalogue tells me the styling of the Classic is based on an amalgam of early 1950s Bullet models (the first swinging arm model was the G2), modern technical necessities and contemporary retro flim-flammery. The press release tells us that part of

the design has been done by British motorcycle styling house Xenophya (who have also done the Mac Motorcyles project) and part in house. The end result being a retro-bike that actually looks like an old bike (*except for the front disk, lack of kick-start and fuel injection: Ed.*). Just for fun I re-registered mine as a 1961 model and put on a black and silver plate (*naughty: Ed.*). This has resulted in endless London cabbies giving me a thumbs-up and mouthing "nice" to me when we stop at lights (I think I might get the old reg. back!).

Continued Page 90

(Left and below)
The Royal Enfield
new Clubman EFI.

*Mr Sean Peschiera wears (one off)
Royal Enfield / Barbour International
jacket modified by the photographer.*

Ms Abby Clee wears vintage Lewis Leathers Plainsman jacket and new Lewis Leathers leather pants. Abbey sits astride a new Royal Enfield Bullet Clubman EFI.

BARBOUR INTERNATIONAL JACKET

(One off) Royal Enfield / Barbour International wax cotton jacket (modified by the photographer).

Original Barbour International wax cotton jacket. This example was supplied to the 1976 British ISDT Team (courtesy Cassie Mercantile).

The café racer version of the Bullet is named the Clubman EFI and does have a kick-start, ace bars, loud exhaust, alloy tank, over-run 'popping' when you throttle back and a lot of charisma. I rode this bike around London and can confirm that it's agile, comfortable and really fun and once again the only slightly annoying thing is the amount of attention you get from other road users and passers-by which means a lot of smiling and saying "thank you" while fielding unsolicited compliments. The nearest thing to this model in today's market is probably the CCM CR-40, a café racer of great beauty and some performance but a foreigner in that special land colonised by the Royal Enfield. This is not a motorway speed machine but still very nippy in traffic and because of this perhaps I can suggest a modern and efficient retro-looking front drum brake?

Continued Page 93

90

Mr Steven Philipson wears (one off) Royal Enfield /
Barbour International wax cotton jacket.

Back pocket detail of 1976 British ISDT jacket
(courtesy Cassie Mercantile).

Above and below: Royal Enfield Trials EFI.

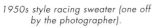

1950s style racing sweater (one off by the photographer).

The Trials EFI could be the best looking of the range if the painted steel tank could be replaced by the same workmanship in alloy allotted to the Clubman. That said, this is still a very stylish and efficient machine, looking at home beside the Standard 10 and Frog-eyed Sprite organised by the photographer for the *Men's File* photo-shoot.

Links

www.royal-enfield.com
www.hitchcocksmotorcycles.com
www.lewisleathers.com
www.barbour.com
www.xenophya.com
www.mac-motorcycles.com
www.cassiemercantile.com

93

Triton: The CP Project

Triton building has become a significant genre within the realm of motorcycle art and there are some really amazing examples in the UK, Europe and the US (just look at Peter Andrews' twin-engined model in Classic Bike, Jan 2010): but anything like this...?

Designed by Vincent Prat (of Southsiders MC) and this is yet another advance in automotive styling it's the historical distance these particular they manipulate and re-form, that seems to builders. Or perhaps it's just that Prat, Consisting of Unit T140 engine (750cc) Featherbed frame, the bike has already (amongst others) so is not, like most of what don't bloody well care (alright?! Ed.). We as possible and we wanted (in a grand way) to Toulouse based photographer who has a very crisp will be more of his work and more unbelievable stuff from France

Frank Charriaut and constructed by Daniel Delfour from France (see Retromobile, page 74). Perhaps Frenchmen have from the British commodities give them the edge on Britsih and American Charriaut and Delfour are very good. with a Tiger single-carb head and Slimline appeared on the Southsiders MC blog we feature, exclusive to *Men's File*, but we wanted to let as many people see this bike introduce the photography of Benoit Guerry, a and precise method of representing machines. There and Southsiders MC in issue 04 of *Men's File*.

southsiders-mc.blogspot.com

More interesting French stuff:

gadget-motorcycles.com   vd-classic.com   brooklands-classic.com   atelier-chatokhine.com   ateliersruby.com

triton-france.com   ton-up.fr   fanakick-motorcycle-club.com   gaillon110ansapres.free.fr

79

The Wall of Death

Photography and text: *Gary Margerum*

A name that strikes terror and wonder? A wall separates and blocks, while death is the ultimate divider. This is a story of old-skool showmen, real riding and real danger. We thrill and admire but fear to lay rubber on those boards. Photographer Gary Margerum did all the work on this so we would prefer our readers hear his account first hand.

The Fox family

Now with Alex and Luke (Ken's sons) riding. The Fox family are entering their fourth generation with the wall of death. The riders are: Ken Fox, Alex Fox (16 years old), Luke Fox (24) and Kerri Cameron (no age – she will kill me) that's Luke's fiancée and Jamie star (17),

42

she started riding May this year. Other regular riders are Danny Dare and Ken Wolfe. With Julie, Ken's wife, keeping things running smoothly. Ken has been riding and performing from 16 years of age and built his own wall in 1994. The whole exercise was completed in just 20 weeks. The wall Ken built back then is still performing today, with running repairs. As well as the wall they also have to maintain the bikes, lorrys and travelling equipment. This of course is done in-house. The Ken Fox troupe is one of the last great travelling shows in Europe. Ken, his wife Julie and their family and friends help to keep this show on the road every year.

MOTORCYCLE
ZOMBIES

Photography and Text: Gabe Sullivan

The Cycle Zombies are a motorcycle crew made up of a family of surfers from Huntington Beach, California. This tight knit group is comprised of Scott Stopnik and his two sons Scotty and "The Turk". Scott Senior makes his living installing dry cleaning machinery. Scotty Junior works for the surf apparel giant Hurley as a brand ambassador and surf team rider. Spending several days a week diligently scouring the local swap meets, thrift stores and auction websites, Scotty is constantly in search of stylish vintage clothing, furniture, surf, skate and motorcycle stuff. He occasionally delivers select pieces to Hurley's designers for inspiration and reference. The rest of his stuff (like the bikes he fixes up) he sells via word of mouth or by listing for sale on their blog (www. czombieblog.com). The younger Stopnik brother is called "Turk" (we still don't know what his real name is) and works at the newly opened Captain's Helm surf shop in Costa Mesa. *Men's File* met up with the trio on a recent Sunday morning in Huntington Beach at their headquarters (Scotty's garage), where this interview took place.

(continued page 59)

58

(continued from p. 56)

Gabe Sullivan: *What's the story behind the Cycle Zombies slogan: Two Wheels, One Fin?*

Scotty Stopnik: Well, me and [my brother] Turk have always ridden a lot of single fins growing up, and since we're known for surfing and riding bikes it just stuck. We will always ride bikes and always ride single fins.

GS: *Did your father [Scott Senior] introduce you and Turk to surfing and bike culture?*

SS: My dad has been around bikes and surfing his whole life. When I was seven, he got me a board and started taking me and Turk to Bolsa Chica State Beach. As we grew up, we would work with him installing dry cleaners and that's where we learned to work with our hands. He told us that even if we didn't work for him forever, we would always have his trade. He was constantly buying and swapping cars and bikes, so we always had something new or different to cruise to the beach with him in. I got an '83 HD Sportster when I was 17, and Turk started working on a Triumph project when he was 15. It's hands down thanks to our Dad for what we have and know.

GS: *Does the family who rides together, stay together?*

SS: Yes we ride together as much as possible and always have our backs and stay true to each other. Blood is thicker than water.

GS: *What happens on Sunday mornings at Rooster Café in Costa Mesa?*

SS: Our good friend Brian Wilson owns the Café and he hosts a vintage motorcycle rally on the first Sunday of every month. It's a killer little joint that has good food and good friends talkin' trash and

checkin' out the latest old find someone rides up on. The food is amazing and I usually get the Early Riser with a side of hashbrowns. It's an egg and bacon sandwich with sourdough bread. I also always get a large Diet Coke, you know, to keep the sperm count up.

GS: *What do you think about surfing, skateboarding and motorcycling seemingly morphing into one 'look' at the moment?*

SS: Surfing, skating and motorcycles are what we're all about. As we started getting the whole Cycle Zombie thing out there with our blog, it started to pick up followers and people were into it. But like always, there will be haters who talk trash and say stuff like: 'surfing, skating and motorcycles don't go together.' But to me, riding bikes is about freedom. Just get on your bike and blast down the road not caring about a thing in the world. It's the same feeling you get when you surf or skate. They all represent freedom and give you a moment to forget about your worries. And yes, Max Schaff and Jason Jessie are two older pro skaters who are probably the most popular people in the motorcycle world. They are heavily into choppers and you always see rad stuff on them in magazines with their bikes and boards.

GS: *How long have you been collecting and how much time do you devote to searching for all this cool stuff you have accumulated in your garage?*

SS: As long as I can remember I was going to swap meets. My dad would take me when I was three years old. Then when I was about 13 or 14, I started riding my bicycle to the swap and started looking for old surf/ skate stuff and illegal weapons to bring home. I got my mom to let me borrow her ID to set

up an eBay account and it was all downhill from there. I'm always looking for cool stuff that catches my eye. Estate sales are on Fridays, swaps on Saturday, Sunday and Monday and trash digging is everyday. I love the swaps and thrift stores. It's really like a treasure hunt and you never know what you'll find. The online stuff for sale is a gold mine as well, you just have to be always searching and keeping up on the hottest items that sell quick.

GS: *What can you tell us about your SkateWing?*

SS: The SkateWing is magical. I was out at this little crappy

swap on a Wednesday morning and while looking at some records this guy pulled the SkateWing out of his car. He bought it earlier in the morning for like $30 and wanted $150 for it. I laughed at him and walked off, but about an hour later it was mine for $75. It wasn't that cheap of a find, but I've never seen one in real life and it's one of those rare boards you just gotta have in the quiver.

www.czombieblog.com
www.eatatrooster.com
www.captainshelm.com
www.crudebehavior.net

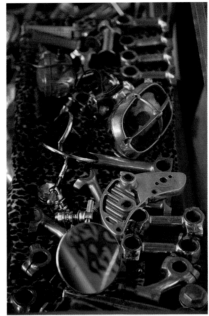

Scotty on the nose. Surf photo: Mark Choiniere.

61

Beaulieu Brough

Photography: *Nick Clements*

Beaulieu is located at the southern edge of the New Forest (in fact a very old forest) near to the English South Coast. The beauty of the area is almost unparalleled, which is why, one suspects, the French for 'beautiful place' was chosen by some long forgotten order of Norman monks who resided at the local abbey. Now the site of the National Motor Museum, each year the hamlet hosts the Netley Marsh autojumble, an acknowledged Mecca for buyers and sellers of everything connected with classic automotive culture. It was on a warm September afternoon that we arrived at the scene in full leathers and original pre-war flannels with the task to seek out the promised JAP engined, Brough MX80.

www.brough-superior.com
www.oldtimer-outfit.com
www.thecurator.co.uk
www.stetson-europe.com

Mr Leonard Rout sports a 1930s replica racing suit by Lewis Leathers.

Mr Jamie Delaney wears his own everyday original pre-war attire.
Brough Superior MX with JAP V-twin loaded by Mark Upham of Brough Superior.

77

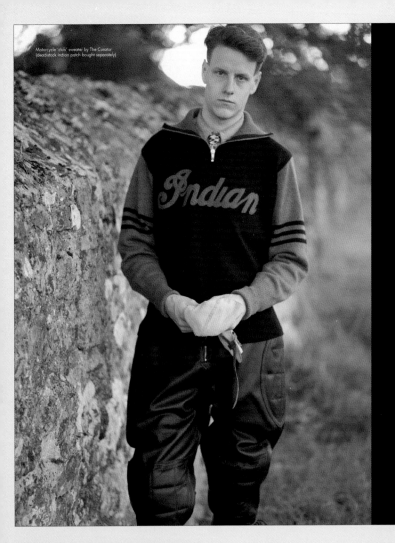

Motorcycle 'club' sweater by The Curator (deadstock Indian patch bought separately)

Original 1930s felt motorcyclist's dust mask and British Army dispatch rider's coat

79

motofile

Racing cap with built-in goggles by Josef Reichensperner.

80

Hat by Stetson.

128

Some cross to bear

Text: *Simon McLean*

At the end of the Second World War, returning GI's, discharged and ruptured, took to restlessly riding the roads of postwar America. The Outlaw Biker had arrived. These ex-GI bikers were the first to openly sport their war trophies, bringing back helmets, belt buckles and Iron Crosses.

First introduced by King Friedrich Wilhelm III, King of Prussia during the Napoleonic Wars, then later adopted by the German Army under Bismarck, this symbol of valour and bravery continued to develop its symbolic meaning, changing with each political twist and turn of the German Reich. Then in the 1930s the medal was appropriated by the Nazis, a swastika was added and became the most prized Third Reich decoration.

Carrying some pretty contaminated baggage, which in part added to its appeal to whole generations of postwar rebels, it gained a new iconic counter-culture significance that in recent years has spilled into the area of commercialisation.

By the early sixties the Iron Cross insignia had become an established element of biker lore, a part of the uniform associated with 'showing class', or 'snapping the citizens minds'. Somehow the Iron Cross differentiated between the greasy biker as a small-time harbinger of impending trouble and the iron-horseman of the apocalypse endorsed by the symbol of the ancient order of Teutonic Knights.

The black and silver four pointed compass of evil, a natural hex, symbolic, geometric, a kind of magnetic biker cross hair, complimented chrome, oily indigo, blackened pistons and burnt rubber, hand in sweaty glove.

Oversized, chromed and glorious, it became the cross of choice for everyone from chain whippin' Angels, Outlaws, Altamont hitters, Peckinpah posters, Kubrick's Billy Boy, salt flat rod knockin' street racin' Roth freaks, tear drop tanks, surf Nazis, and Pistol Punks out to shock. Leaving a searing visual legacy, littering the work of such as Danny Lyons, Hunter S Thompson, Karl Heinz Weinberger et al.

Does the Iron Cross still threaten with mystery and meaning, or is it lost in its subversion and misappropriation, or is it just a rusty old piece of iron?

"This stuff - the iron crosses, the Nazi insignia, the German helmets – that's to shock people. To let 'em know we're individualists. To let 'em know we're Angels" (Sonny Barger)

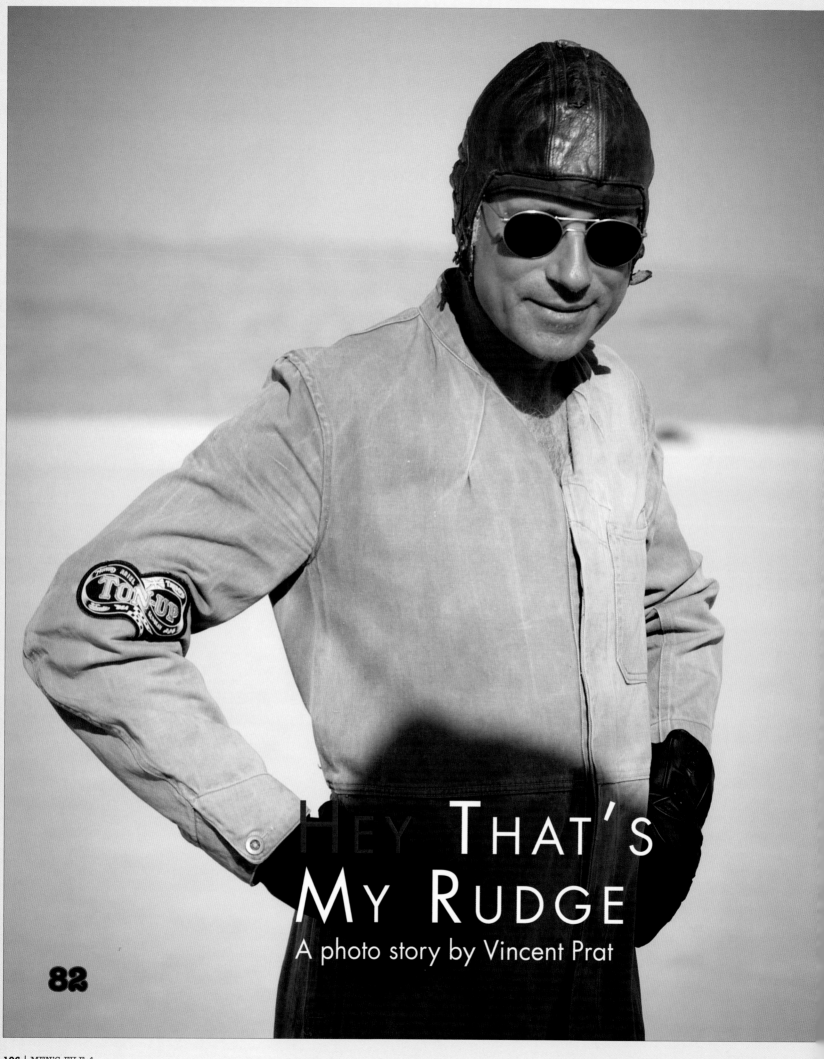

Hey That's My Rudge

A photo story by Vincent Prat

This is Jean-Claude Barrois. He's 52 years old, lives in the middle of France at Chateauneuf sur Charente and for twenty-five years has been fascinated by Burt Munro's epic story. In the summer of 2009 he finished his highly modified 1927 Rudge and turned his sights to Bonneville 2010.

Jean-Claude, is a true revivalist living every single day as if it were in the 1920s, he concentrates on ancient mechanical cultures and an automotive way of life. Despite not speaking English the tall Frenchman's natural command of the universal language of mechanical engineering meant he was immediately adopted by the 'speed' community camped on the dry floor of a primeval lake, now used as a savage testing ground for man and machine. For his first year on the Salt Flats, his goal wasn't a record attempt but simply participation. He made several runs along the black line but retired due to fuelling and camshaft problems. Now hooked on 'salt' monsieur Barrois and his Rudge will be back at Speedweek for 2011.

PARIS BROUGH

8am. October 23. 2010. We assemble under Pont de la Tournelle, a modernist edifice constructed in 1928 and featuring a monumental sculpture by Paul Landowski. Paris is already the universal stage from which so much great theatre is played out and it seems that this bridge was built with the sole intention of providing a tableaux for a trio of Brough Superior motorcycles to simply exist. This is a three dimensional space where these machines can breathe and rest.

An engine fires-up and the Pendine SS101E Brough (built 2009) departs at some considerable speed, under the bridge and along the pavé along the Seine towards Ile de la Cité. Those not involved in the launch of the beast look around confused. Has it been stolen? Two men, Simon Delany and his son Jamie drag on filterless cigarettes, dressed in their standard post war wardrobe, they talk among themselves. Like the Broughs, in this environment they need only exist to be an integral part of this scene. The sound of a distant exhaust that quickly comes closer and Mr Paul d'Orleans (aka The Vintagent), helmetless, negotiates the cobbles and suicide shift to reappear through the bridge's perfect arc, only a faint grin hints at a three minute adventure about which we can only speculate.

Our purpose here is to photograph the four Brough Superiors and a small part of the Double RL men's clothing range. A dispatch rider's rubberized cotton mac, a tweed jacket, a French casque (cap) and a leather coat. For these items this is also the correct domain as this is where they always belonged.

132

Brough Superior, Pendalpine, based on the 1926 SS100 (2008).

Brough Superior, Pendine SS101E (2008).

Brough Superior, Pendalpine, based on the 1926 SS100 (2008).

All Broughs courtesy of Mark Upham of Brough Superior.
www.brough-superior.com

Rubberized cotton dispatch rider's coat by Double RL.
The Basil Brough, reconstructed 2008 and based on the 1928 Brough Superior.

135

Leather coat with sheepskin collar by Double RL.

136

Tweed jacket, Fair Isle pullover, shirt and tie, all by Double RL.

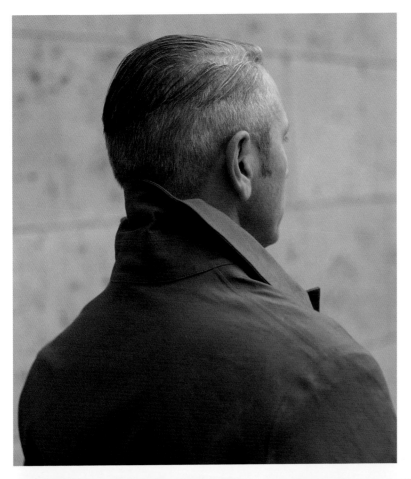

Brough Superior, Lawrence of Arabia SS100 replica (2010).

Holdall bag by Double RL.

139

profile

WITHIN ALL SUBCULTURES there are sub-groups. Since the 1950s sociologists focused on those for whom the subcultural group acts as an alternative family or a medium through which they can rebel against the stifling expectations of the working-class family and social structures. Whether these prosaic definitions are accurate is a matter for conjecture; however, these are not areas of investigation addressed by *Men's File*. We are not interested in rebellion or being part of a community, we are focused purely on style and the individual stylists who have emerged from subcultures and are continuing a work in progress.

We are in a new era in which the ability to communicate across continents at the touch of a button, combined with the universally accepted primacy of the market, has meant a new world of possibilities for those born with the dandy gene. Pure style is blind. It is neither political nor social and avoids unnecessary confrontations as these often lead to the kind of scrutiny that runs counter to the covert approach of the subcultural stylist. The people featured in the pro-file pages do not seek attention from wider society but do 'their thing' for themselves and no one else. If that means producing a product that they would want to wear or use and that others would want to buy – then they have a business.

Revival style still continues to confound the fashion establishment. They simply don't get it and I'm not sure this can be explained in a single paragraph but the foundations of revival, heritage, vintage (call it what you will) fashion come from three rich sources. The first was born in the aftermath of punk and new wave in the late 1970s, when those movements had already pointed the way to a revival of mid-century style, and the other two from the worlds of collecting and auto-cultures. Here we spotlight a collection of stylists, all of whom have journeyed through subculture and have now found themselves at the edge of commodification. By the time this is printed they will have already moved on and side-stepped the clutches of the consumerist machine.

48

Ryan Morris

No one knows where he came from, who his family are, when he was born (or hatched), how he learned to skate so well or play the guitar and perform like a young stage god. We've not even sure if Ryan Morris is even his real name.

Ryan speaks in a language only understood by stoned DJ's in Southern California, oh yes, he used to have his own radio show in Santa Barbara, and a select crew in the Lower East Side skate and fixed gear bike community. He's a goddamn enigma.

We don't know how he gets money to buy his daily bread and although he is selected by photographers, like a painter selects a blank canvas, to perform in some of the most stylish editorial and advertising campaigns around: he's not a professional model. What we do know about the Californian is that his favourite skateboard move is a 'switch heel flip' and the skater he's most influenced by is Louie Barletta. He has been playing the guitar since fifth grade (12 years old) and writes a lot of his own stuff. He visits the Jesus de la Ruiz Gallery when he can and eats often at Marlow and Sons on Broadway and Wythe (Williamsberg).

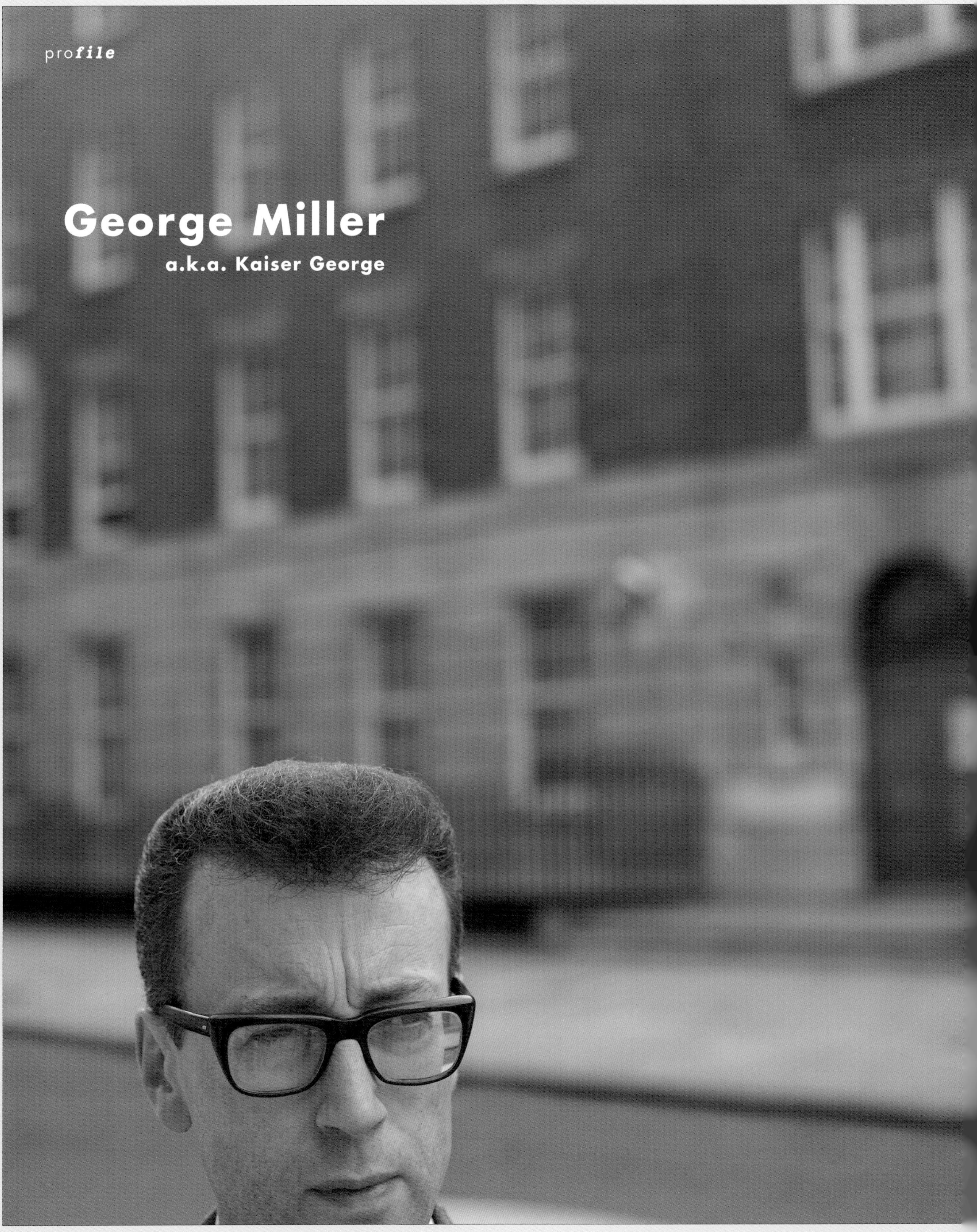

George Miller
a.k.a. Kaiser George

Men's File asked musician and collector George Miller about his personal choice of dress and how he views classic style.

GM: For me, 'classic' style, specifically from the early sixties, has the most appealing design principles of any period before or since. It's based quite strictly on the proportions and lines of the body and there are literally no frills, enhancing the natural silhouette rather than adding to it in the way flared or baggy trousers do. It looks like it means business, without appearing aggressive. There's also a perceived element of "squareness" to it that I quite like, which it seems to be losing slightly with the current popularity of ties, v-neck sweaters and cardigans. I'm sure it'll return soon enough.

Men's File: Where does Mr Miller find such interesting attire?

GM: I used to get my clothes mainly from charity/vintage clothes shops. The charity shops aren't much of a source now, so I use e-bay quite a lot, mainly for ties and cufflinks. Amazingly, there's a fair amount of wearable stuff in high street shops such as Top Man at the moment, especially shoes and trousers. Office usually has some nice chisel toe shoes. The now sadly gone Hardy Amies shops were great for penny and tab collar shirts. I managed to stock up before they closed and I like them so much I never wear anything else shirt-wise. I get my boots from Beatwear in Liverpool who do a nice line in Anello & Davide style boots, but cheaper. I sometimes find stuff in Armstrong's Vintage Clothing in Edinburgh and Mr Ben or Retro in Glasgow. If I'm on tour, I'll usually sniff out the local vintage shops. I like British and continental stuff more than American gear, which looks at it's best when worn in America.

Men's File: What about his musical career?

GM: I'm currently playing guitar with Sharleen Spiteri's band and have been in various groups over the years. I started learning guitar in the late seventies, inspired by the early Beatles and Punk Rock. I was in a group called the Styng-Rites which was adopted by the Psychobilly crowd in the '80s and more recently the Kaisers, a staunchly antiquated early '60s beat combo. The Kaisers recorded all their LPs at Toe-Rag Studios in London, a haven for fans of vintage recording techniques. I've also played in a few Rock 'n' Roll groups and had a brief stint in the Revillos when they re-formed some years ago. I'm planning to set up a recording studio when I find suitable premises. I have a home studio, but it's getting rather out of hand. I'm more into the production side of music these days, but will continue to write and record my own stuff when time allows.

Links

www.myspace.com/cgfmguy
www.beatwear.co.uk

*pro**file***

Steven Phillipson

There is no specific name or label that can be placed on the subculture revivalist. Can we call Steven Phillipson a Ton-up Boy, a Rocker, a Greaser? He is a modern man with modern ideas and we are delighted to have him on the pages of this magazine because of his modern style.

S teven is pictured here with his trusty Norton steed at Goodwood and is currently building a 500cc Norton Dommiracer based on a 600cc version by Paul Dunstall. Now 30, Mr Phillipson started taking a serious interest in classic motorcycles at the age of 15. Living for British bikes and the open road Steven is very much part of the contemporary café racer scene having worked at Dave Degens Dresda Racing and Dave Goddard's out on the old A4. Like many of us, this leather clad road warrior has been influenced by the romance of the café brotherhood imparted to him by his father and uncle Mick who frequented all the major West London cafes of that golden era of British bikes. Still riding and still building bikes I hope to see Steven at one of his tea stops (Brits and Pieces, Burgess Hill?) this summer.

Links

www.woodgate.org/dunstall/index.html
www.dresda.co.uk
www.ace-cafe-london.com

53

54

Brian Bent

This is a man of extraordinary energy. Surfer, musician, artist, hot rod builder, San Onofre local and pastor of the Hot Rod Church for Sinners based at Mission Viejo, California. Mr Bent's church offers those with greased quiffs and a set of hot vintage wheels a place to worship amongst fellow devotees of hopped-up machines that also share a love of Jesus.

Brian is seen here with his newly built 1927 Oakland Racer and a hollow wood construction surfboard known as a 'kook-box'. This style of water machine, which was used as a paddle-board and surfboard, was pioneered by swimmer and all round waterman Tom Blake in the

late 1920s and early 1930s. Blake surfed in Hawaii and Southern California and applied for the first US patent for a hollow construction surfboard in 1929. Blake was also the first to put a fin on a craft intended to aid control whilst on the wave. Brian Bent's Kook-box was recently built by Steve Lalonde and is now being campaigned by the churchman at his local break.

The legend on the top of the board 'Roar In Ace' was painted on by Brian.

Some might be surprised by the cool Christian's calling to Jesus and to the waves but remember the Lord lived and worked by water, his friends were fishermen and it's through baptism by water that the sinner can be washed away and the new person be re-born.

The photographs were taken by another San Onofre local and founder of the Old Guys Rule surfwear brand; Mr Don Craig.

Links

www.oldguysrule.com
www.hotrodchurch.com

(Above) Mr Bent and his kook box get in the slot on a friendly San Onofre swell (spring, 2009). (Right) A mid-century modern interior by Brian Bent (2000).

DAVID NOLAN

A London based fashion stylist whose clients include Italian magazine *L'Uomo Vogue* and Savile Row tailors Gieves & Hawkes, Mr David Nolan is a lifelong admirer of classic style in all its guises. Before entering the fickle arena of fashion, Mr Nolan worked in the real world of the automotive industry until 2003, jacking it in for an intensive year at the London College of Fashion. The stylist's first solo photo-shoot was at the 2005 British Bike Bonanza, a premier vintage scramble meeting in Gloucestershire. We consider *Men's File* readers to be those who buy each item of clothing with much care and consideration and would never seek to 'advise' on what, when and how to wear anything, however we value Mr Nolan's opinion and have reproduced in this profile a short interview.

Men's File: David, you are at the centre of the fashion business and are constantly presented with new styles to evaluate in terms of their relevance to contemporary fashion trends. How does classic style fit into your life?

DN: Perhaps because of what you say about fashion trends I tend to search out the classic lines for myself no matter what is happening in contemporary fashion. For me, a piece of clothing that has classic style is something that will always hold up on its own, and maintain a lasting appeal regardless of trends or fashion. I've always felt fashion and style to be very separate things. Fashion usually tends to create something that can quite quickly lose its appeal and relevance. Genuinely great style and design will always stand the test of time and make an item of clothing become a classic, being just as relevant now as when it was first introduced. Some items of clothing just never date: a great raincoat, a Harrington jacket or a classic suit. Just look at images of Alain Delon in a raincoat, Elvis Presley wearing a Harrington, or Sebastian Flyte (*from Brideshead Revisited: Ed.*) wearing any number of beautiful suits. Their style has just as much resonance and allure today as it had back then, irrespective of the passing of the decades.

What David Nolan chooses to wear

A Rain coat: *Always Burberry for a classic rain coat.*
Harrington jacket: *Baracuta. Worn by Elvis Presley, Steve McQueen, The Clash etc.*
Brogues, Derbies: *Trickers or Churches ready made, or Lobb for bespoke.*
Shirts: *Margaret Howell for effortless quality.*
Leather jackets: *Lewis Leathers for cut, quality and absolute timeless style.*
Boots: *Carol Christian Poell or Guidi. More contemporary but absolute investments and without a doubt future classics.*
Tailoring: *Gieves & Hawkes and Dunhill for off the peg or bespoke. Totally classic, effortless, elegant tailoring.*
Denim: *always Levi's. One of the oldest and most iconic denim brands, timeless.*
Knitwear: *John Smedley: Best quality and still making from their mills since 1700's.*

25

WORKSHOP:

An insight into the process of making.

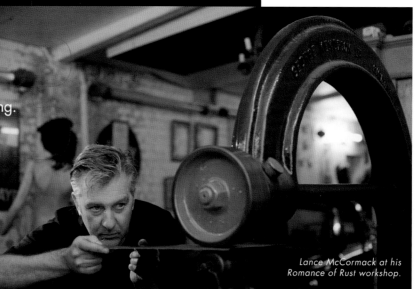

Lance McCormack at his Romance of Rust workshop.

Romance of Rust: The workshop of Mr Lance McCormack

Location: West Ealing, London.

Lance McCormack is a metal fabricator operating at the highest level. It's not just about the skill of manipulating sheet steel, it's about translating the needs of the client into a finished product that astonishes in terms of quality of make and aesthetic tone. If you go to Lance with a XK120 bonnet that needs to be louvered, he will do it in the required style, be that traditional or modern. If you want a strip cut out the roof of your chopped lead-sled and a section invisibly placed into that gaping hole with the name of the car embossed into the replacement section: call Mr McCormak. We think you understand.

www.romanceofrust.co.uk

O35

Sixth Street Specials:
The workshop of Mr Hugh Mackie

Location: E. 6th Street, NYC.

Mr Mackie is really building some special British bikes for hip New Yorkers in the East Village bike scene. A graduate of the Glasgow School of Art, the Scot migrated to New York in the mid-1980s and soon found his calling restoring British twins. The most desirable bike to have today must be a well set-up British flat-tracker/ street-tracker, and Hugh Mackie is a master of this genre. He's not bad at setting up SR400/500s too.

Mark Powell's Workshop

Photography: *Nathan Small*

Here we visit the Frith Street work-space of raconteur, designer and Soho 'face' Mr. Mark Powell.

Since the mid-1980s there are many who have granted themselves the title of 'tailor' and over the years some have remained and triumphed. The talented ones have consistently produced beautifully crafted garments in the classic style but with an element of their own style added. This is the essence of 'classic with a twist' – a very 1980s concept – that is the trademark of many a contemporary thimble-smith. Just to be clear – Mark Powell is not in this group and in our view he is in a category of his own.

Since 1989 Mr Powell has selected the very best of the past seventy years of men's formal wear (suits, jackets, overcoats and shirts) and somehow re-cut and re-worked here and there in a way that confuses the fashion historian. This magician of the cloth delights those who we might describe as Dandies, New Edwardians, Ivy Leaguers or Sartorialists.

There is a long line of movie stars and celebrities on his client list but *Men's File* is not impressed. We just care about the clothes and the moods that Mark Powell evokes with his designs and nobody we are aware of has surpassed him. Can you afford it? A bespoke suit is for those who have money and simply love to have perfectly fitted clothing. On the more reasonable side: if you want a snap-tab penny-collar shirt that looks like it came straight from the neck of Charlie Watts in 1963 then pay Mark a visit.

www.markpowellbespoke.co.uk

37

ASHLEY LLOYD-JENNINGS

A Collector and Arbiter of Taste

Photography: *Matt Hind*
Still-life Photography: *George Ong*
Text: *David Lees*

Ashley Lloyd-Jennings is best known for starting the traditional men's clothing brand Hackett with Jeremy Hackett in 1983, but the story does not start there. Leaving the RAF in 1963 ALJ set up a small men's boutique called Gentry in his hometown of Bournemouth, with most items sourced wholesale from Carnaby Street entrepreneur John Stephen. Gentry stocked salmon pink Newman jeans and needle cord button down shirts aiming to be "something completely mental that would bring a little bit of what London was about" to the sleepy seaside town.

66

ALJ's move to London, saw him DJ'ing at the Embassy Club, opening the city's first revival Art Deco store on the Portobello Road in 1967 with Carlo Manzi (now a well known film costumier) and then learning his trade managing numerous stores for other people. In 1979 ALJ opened Lloyd-Jennings, an eponymous shoe shop in Covent Garden on Neal Street selling high quality, hand lasted, men's shoes. At a time when formal footwear was hard to find in London, the Neal Street store acquired a dedicated clientele including the crown heads of Belgium, Jordan and Spain.

Apart from persuading the classic American shoe manufacturer Alden to produce their beautiful hand stitched tassel loafer for his Lloyd-Jennings shops, ALJ was the first in Europe to stock the now ubiquitous Sperry Topsider boating shoe. Bass Loafers were also a staple of the store.

In the post-loons / pre-Punk period (1973 – 77) there was little on offer for the slightly eccentric, dapper British man. A follow-on from Skinhead culture (catered for by The Ivy Shop in Richmond), a Teddy Boy revival, Glam-Rock and Anthony Price perhaps filled a void for a few but most interesting style was way beneath the radar with pockets of fashion or music based subculture here and there and not much else. What did emerge in parallel with Punk was 'revival' which meant second hand clothing becoming currency for individuals who wanted something different. High quality American vintage stuff was rare (Johnson's in Kensington Market and the Kings Road did some interesting replica apparel after '79) but there was a seam

of pristine, well cared for English tailoring out there that was largely untapped. This was the beginnings of a 'market' and it was this imaginative retailer who saw that opportunity.

The first Hackett store was opened down the unfashionable end of the Kings Road in 1983, a joint venture with Jeremy Hackett. They specialised in finding second hand English formal menswear and selling it for a tidy profit to the sons of the English gentry (and some council house gits too). With the first New King's Road shop, demand outstripped supply and the partners started sourcing traditional manufacturers to produce their own take on off the peg English tailoring. Hackett became a phenomenon. The brand made such an impact that it was the first menswear range to occupy all the display windows on Barney's 5th Avenue store. But it was the diffusion ranges, carrying the St. Georges Cross, with an unabashed "Englishness" that became popular on the football terraces and core customers were alienated. Alfred Dunhill bought Hackett in the early 90's. The sale eventually resulted in ALJ on the board of the Richemont Group. There he was given the freedom to express his love of style on a grand scale and was instrumental in the group's acquisition of Purdy, Panerai and Old England (Paris' nod to Anglo style).

Today ALJ spends his time between London and Morocco and has retained much of his retail history, based on his personal taste, in the form of an extensive shoe collection. Custom made Bass Weejun's, Alden loafers and examples from the Lloyd-Jennings shoe store era have all been photographed and displayed in this magazine as a homage to a collector and great arbiter of taste.

A small sample of Ashley Lloyd-Jenning's shoe collection as it exists today.

67

Conrad's Studio

Photography: Nathan Small

Based in London, Mr Conrad Leach is a self taught painter / illustrator producing highly stylised interpretations of the motorcycle at speed (and other associated imagery). *Men's File* did an email interview with this busy man, which we hope will add insight to these shots of his studio. Conrad sets out his stall for all to see when he describes his influences as "a combination of European, American and Japanese culture" and adds "I am really inspired by the global cross fertilization taking place in the custom bike world at the moment". From our perspective he has mixed the graphic languages of the 1930s and 40s illustrators like Geo Ham with some more contemporary Kar Kulture styles to create a vibrant and dynamic effect that is very much his own and is reflected in an impressive list of solo exhibitions.

Conrad Leach

Like many of us, Mr Leach emerged from the Punk years looking for inspiration and "was caught up in the revivalist culture for the 1950s and 60's" going on to say "the things I discovered seemed much more exotic than modern life, as it was then". Also, like *Men's File* he is not dogmatic in his adherence to pure revival style and states in the clearest terms "I am now most interested in the combination of modern and retro aesthetic". Yes, Conrad, we at *Men's File* also like to take the best from both worlds.

You can purchase many of his images as prints in limited editions of 30. We suggest looking on his website for more information on exhibitions and print sales.

conradleach.com

33

Mr Freedom! Photography and text: *Matt Hind*

Christophe Loiron has operated Mister Freedom, his heritage inspired concept, out of his 7161, Beverley Boulevard location since 2003. A treasure trove of found vintage clothing and accessories the building is also the headquarters for his own original clothing line, the result of a collaboration with the Tokyo based manufacturer Sugar Cane Co. *Men's File* caught up with him last October to find out how it all started.

"I travelled all over the place growing up, mainly around Africa: Ivory Coast, Tchad, Zaire, Djibouti... Wanderlust. Put some sand in my shoes. Was dreaming all along about America. Most of my early influences originated in the USA, music, styles, movies... At twentyfour I made it to California. I had a guitar and a small suitcase. No goal if not just to prove I could fly with my own wings (you know, just to show Dad...) and maybe eventually visit Sun Records Studio in Memphis! Been here in LA ever since. California's sand is good, and the grass is greener to me.

I started hunting down vintage stuff as a way of paying bills, keeping alive my childhood fling for treasure hunting and junk collecting. In the US, early 90s, it was still out there, ready to be picked. Those days were fun and exciting. You could find unbelievable things that most times didn't mean anything to whoever owned it. They were happy to get rid of it, you were beyond thrilled to find it and drive it back in a loaded 24 footer from Texas to LA. Spent a lot of time in rat infested rag houses, going through bins of ready-to-cut rags, and find the most amazing old patched up 'hobo' denim, sun-faded sweats etc, ready to get chopped... sold by the pound. I also collected old clothing labels and buttons from those 'trash bins'. After seeing all that, getting ideas for future designs was easy... just needed to keep the mental photos organized".

"...I try to create things that didn't exist but could have, so I stay away from replicas. I create clothes the way I would like to find them on the shelves. "New Old Stock" style, not using distressing gimmicks and polluting washes. The reason they 'look old' is the result of a mix of sewing techniques, fabrics, styles, packaging. They may as well be some dead stock garments from 70 years ago..."

The Mister Freedom Sugar Cane Spring Summer 2011 collection is a bit of a departure for Christophe and his American love affair. "Les Apaches" takes its name and spirit from the French slang for the dandy gangsters of the Parisian Belle Époque. Using early French fabrics and details it mixes plaids and stripes, bold colours and small calico prints and while Christophe knows the California sand in his boots is there to stay, this nod to his Gallic origins will keep things interesting.

7161 Beverly Boulevard, Los Angeles
California 90036 USA
www.misterfreedom.com

16

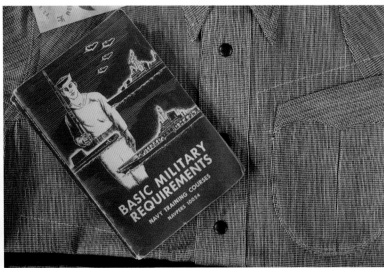

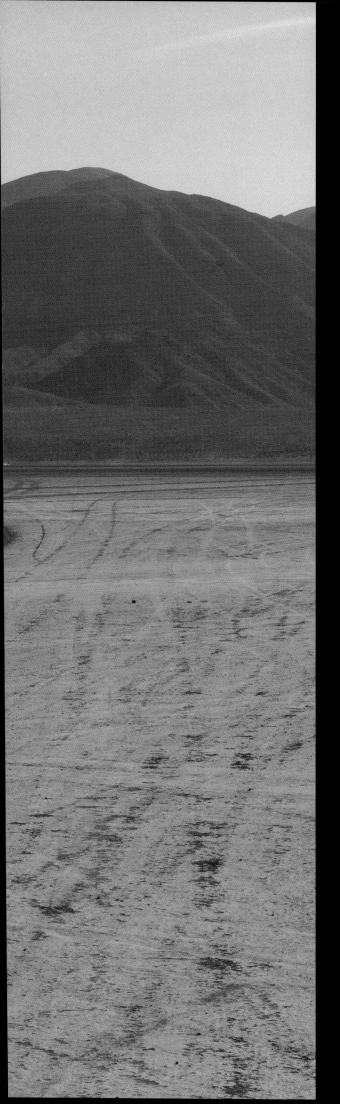

endeavourfile

IT HAS BEEN the brief of *Men's File* to chronicle our times in terms of style and the older male. We couldn't do everything, so we concentrated on exceptional individuals who often combined considerable talent with much imagination in terms of personal presentation. They come from different fields but they can all be called 'stylists'.

The surfer who decides to 'zig' when everyone else is 'zagging' – in every sense of the term – is the currency of *Men's File*. In a world that dictates sameness, while calling it individuality, there seem to be few young people prepared to go against the crowd. It takes courage to be different as we are all afraid of being on some sort of blacklist that we neither understand or ever get to see.

In these pages we see a group of pioneering surfers, skateboarders, soapbox cart builders, cricket bat makers and mountain climbers who brave the high peaks in traditional tweeds. The representation of such endeavour is perfectly illustrated by the work of the intrepid photographers and writers who sought them out and got the features to us. Producing *Men's File* is a journey of discovery for the staff as much as for the readers. The stylists continue to amaze and entertain and long may that continue.

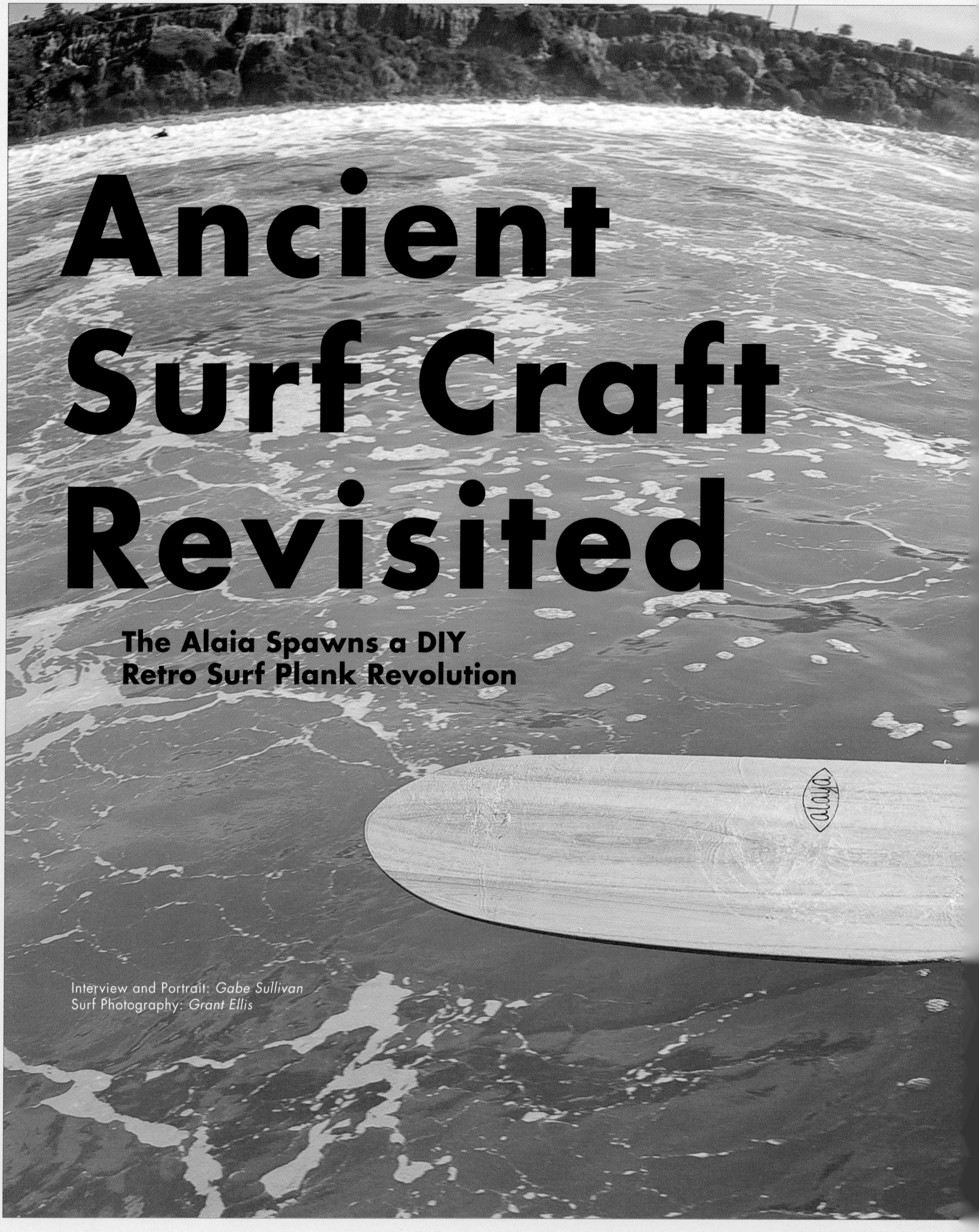

Ancient Surf Craft Revisited

The Alaia Spawns a DIY Retro Surf Plank Revolution

Interview and Portrait: *Gabe Sullivan*
Surf Photography: *Grant Ellis*

Rob Machado shows how to
surf on a wooden plank.

09

All About the Alaia

Riding an alaia surfboard might seem a bit like choosing to travel via horse and carriage in the midst of today's motorized world of sleek and souped up cars. But the alaia offers more than the novelty of riding an elegant and minimalist piece of surf history—these boards really do go really fast. The trick is figuring out how to successfully add one to your quiver. Tom Wegener sells his alaia surfboards to just a few select surf shops and fulfills only a handful of custom orders. "Making alaias" says Wegener, "is a craft that cannot be manufactured for mass production."

Seems like the best way to go might be to shape your own alaia. In fact, now that Wegener is selling alaia blanks—and with a little DIY chutzpah—it's possible to do just that. Wegener began getting bombarded with emails asking where to source the paulownia wood he uses to make his boards and for information on making alaias. "In the past, I wanted to sell more blanks but the costs were too high," said Wegener. "Finally, I've found a mill that can supply alaia blanks for a very reasonable cost."

The blanks are made of the harder species of paulownia, which is best for thin alaias. The lengths are glued together and will not come apart in salt water. The sheets are 19-20mm thick, 17.5 inches wide and up to 7 feet 11 inches long.

"Selling blanks is a bit of a new tack from selling finished surfboards," said Wegener, "but I think this is important for two reasons: First, I'm worried the alaia movement may stall if people

cannot get their hands on good boards. Many people are interested in the boards, but few surfers have actually seen one. Second, there is something very satisfying about making your own board. You get a real connection with your board and the surfing universe when you've faced a block of raw material and made a surfboard."

The tools you need to shape an alaia are very basic. When ordering a blank, Wegener supplies a paper template, which can be drawn onto the board. The template can be altered according to personal preference. A hand saw is all you need to cut out the board. To shape the board, a very sharp jack plane and sand paper are needed. The process does take some time, so patience is required. Keep in mind that the ancients did it with hand tools, using much harder wood. A very small, inexpensive power planer will make the job easier. Electric sanders are helpful as well, however a sanding block and variety of grits of fresh sand paper will also work.

The blanks are already the perfect thickness to be surfed well—in fact even if the board is barely shaped at all, it can still be ridden. The board can also be re-shaped many times. "I've often reshaped a board several times to feel how the board changes," said Wegener. "That's how you really learn a lot about alaia shapes."

Links

www.wegenersurfboards.com
www.tomwegenersurfboards.com

INTERVIEW: ROB MACHADO ON THE ALAIA

Gabe Sullivan: *What type of boards have you been riding lately?*

Rob Machado: I like to dabble in different surfboards—no doubt about that. Lately I've been playing around on these alaia surfboards that Tom Wegener has been making. I believe it's a copy of an ancient Hawaiian surfboard that he found in the Bishop Museum. He kind of added his little twists here and there—a little concave—I'm sure those boards didn't have concave back in the day. Basically it's just a plank of wood—looks like an ironing board or a bookshelf with a rounded off nose and no rocker and no fin. I guess you could call it a surfboard. But it's really just a piece of wood. But it's really fun. It's also really challenging and difficult to ride. But when you get a good wave and you feel the glide and flow it gives you—it's a pretty amazing feeling.

GS: *What's it like to paddle and duck dive the alaia?*

RM: The buoyancy isn't quite there. You duck dive and it takes you twice as long to come up—so you find yourself underwater for a long time. It's pretty interesting. I was surfing Uluwatu on it without a leash and that pretty much sucked. You know, there were a couple fun moments but for the most part I had to do that dead low tide reef walk while my board was smashing into

reef. But it was all good; looking back now, it was fun. It was a good experience.

GS: *What about the speed factor compared to conventional boards?*

RM: You get crazy glide on the alaia, just effortless. You just stand there—it's pretty neat. I like to ride all kinds of boards. I just rode this little 5'4" [Channel Islands] Fishcuit board yesterday—little quad fin with a swallow tail. Really fast and fun.

GS: *Have you ever tried to surf on something that wasn't designed to be ridden on a wave? Like a table or door?*

RM: For Taj [Burrow's] movie Fair Bits we had a little day of filming up in LA somewhere and brought pretty much everything and anything down to the beach and tried to ride it. I actually caught a wave on a guitar case. I couldn't quite stand up—I was pretty close but I rode it like a boogie board and got fully barreled. It was pretty funny.

Rob Machado takes a break while filming on location in Bali, Indonesia for his upcoming surf movie, The Drifter.

08

Dave
Hackett

Brad
Bowman

Skateboard Daddy

Photography: *Gabe Sullivan*

LEGENDS OF SKATE

With Over 150 Years Of Collective
Skateboarding Experience Between
Them, These Men Are Still Riding Fast
And Taking Chances In The Deep End.

Steve
Olson

Lance
Mountain

A group of legendary California skateboarders including Christian Hosoi, Lance Mountain, Steve Olson, Dave Hackett and Brad Bowman recently got together for a shred session in John O'Shei's backyard bowl in Malibu. O'Shei designed his curvy bowl to emulate the Southern California skate parks of the '70's and '80's—and it proved to be the perfect terrain for this group of seasoned masters who've been skating for 30 plus years each.

09

Gabe Sullivan: How does the Malibu Bowl compare to the original California skate parks from back in the '70's & '80's?

Lance Mountain: The shallow end is a more modern take, but pretty much what we all grew up on at that time.

GS: What is the inspiration behind your paintings seen here?

LM: They came from the pictures I had on my wall from Skateboarder Magazine of the boys. I painted them in a style that evolved out of my son's drawings from when he was four. I would paint over his scribbles and then my paintings moved into their own style. After I ran out of his drawings, I started recreating that look with other images.

Christian Hosoi

Lance Mountain

Lance Mountain

Dave Hackett

Christian Hosoi

Steve Olson

GS: What was your favorite aspect of this session at the Malibu Bowl?

Dave "Hackman" Hackett: My favorite aspect of sessioning the Malibu Bowl that day was and always is, riding with my bro's Olson, Bowman, Hosoi and Lance. We've all been riding pools for over 30 years and there is magic that happens when we all get together.

GS: How rare is it for this group of guys to get together?

DH: It's kinda rare—while I see most of these guys individually at events, openings and secret pool sessions, to get all of us together in one pool is epic.

GS: What is it about skateboarding that keeps you doing it?

DH: The feeling of ultimate freedom. It's like flying on the ground. It's like surfing cement. The aspect of danger is always present and I'm an adrenaline junkie.

GS: What influence does surfing have on your skating?

DH: Surfing influences every aspect of my skateboarding; in fact, I really don't ever see what I'm riding through the eyes of a skateboarder—I see a wave and I'm surfing every time I step onto my skateboard.

GS: Have you always skated with the bandana hanging out of your back pocket?

DH: No, not always. I started doing that about 32 years ago.

Lance Mountain

John O'Shei

Steve Olson

Brad Bowman

Christian Hosoi

Dave Hackett

Lance Mountain

Brad Bowman

Wardrobe: *Cindy Whitehead*
Wardrobe assistant: *Adrienne Oliverie*
Photography assistant: *Christian Yeager*
Production: *Brad Bowman*

Fashion Credits

Page 08   **Dave Hackett**
Fedora hat by Hurley.
Aviator sunglasses by Ray Ban.
Iron Cross necklace by Tony Creed.
Button-down shirt by Dolce & Gabbana.
Jeans by Hurley.

Brad Bowman
Zip-up jacket by Kenneth Cole.
Argyle sweater, grey button-down
shirt and denim jeans all by H&M.
Glasses by Oakley.
Straw fedora hat by Billabong.

Page 09   **Steve Olson**
Western shirt by H Bar C.
Helmet by Black Leather Racing.
Goggles by First Infantry Division.
Leopard scarf by Norma Kamali.
Tortoiseshell sunglasses from
a Beverly Hills pharmacy.

Lance Mountain
Vintage V-neck sweater.
T-shirt by Nike/Vintage hat.

Page 12   **Christian Hosoi**
Paisley t-shirt by Vans.
Vintage felt hat.
Watch by Nixon.
Jeans by Quiksilver.

Page 13   **Steve Olson**
Aviator sunglasses from a
Melrose Ave. street vendor.
Button-down shirt by Silver
Spur Western Wear.
Vintage denim jeans by Slappy Custom.
Shoes by Converse Chuck Taylor.

38

Millichamp and Hall
Traditional Cricket Bat Makers

Hiding behind the Somerset Cricket Club in Taunton is a small 19th century industrial premises, the home of bespoke cricket bat makers Millichamp and Hall. Proprietor and chief "pod shaver" Robert Chambers is a dynamic 30 something who after completing his apprenticeship purchased the company from the original owners Jonathan Hall and Julian Millichamp in 1999. Staying true to his roots, Robert continues to make beautiful cricket bats using traditional techniques.

Willow clefts, the starting point for all bat makers, are supplied by Essex based J.S.Wright and Sons (willow merchants since 1894). All willow supplied is sourced in the U.K. from a straight and quick growing willow called Salix Alba Coerulea (not the romantic weeping willow) and harvested after 12-15 years of growth. The clefts, after seasoning for 9-12 months are then sawn to a workable size and pressed. Before shaping begins, a handle of Sarawak cane is fitted. Interlined in the cane are 3 seams of Malaysian rubber, an effective damper to vibrations caused by the impact of a cricket ball at 90 miles an hour! The bats to be are then stored in a dehumidifier for 2 weeks.

The shaping process consists of an initial shaving with a deadly looking double-handed drawknife then planing with a block plane. The shoulders of the bat are worked with a spoke shave and the handle rasped. All the edges are hand finished with a horse's shinbone and the bat is finally soaked in linseed oil. The bat is then subjected to the violent treatment of knocking-in. Taking the form of a young apprentice bashing the hell out of the face of the bat with a wooden mallet for anything up to one and a half hours.

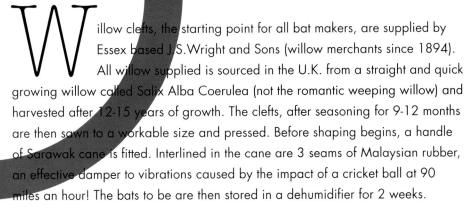

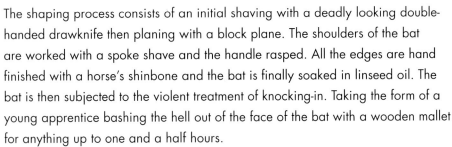

Accommodating cricketing icons (such as Justin Langer and Sachin Tendulkar) as well as keen club players, Robert makes 6 bats a day and altogether the team produce 1500 bats a year. Taking this into account it is easy to understand why a bat of this pedigree will sell for between £150-£300. Millichamp and Hall also offer a rare bespoke service where customers can chose their own cleft and work closely with Robert.

The bat photographed (Right) with a retro inspired design was made especially for *Men's File* and really is a thing to behold.

www.millichampandhall.co.uk

auto*file*

Photography: *Neal Reed*

HotRod Hayride Soapbox Derby

The organisers of the annual Hotrod Hayride shun publicity. We understand why – The Hayride wants participants and not spectators – but we find it difficult not to place Neal Reed's excellent shot of a speeding soapbox at the summer's premier British kar kulture event. There's real racing (cars as well as soapboxes), live music and a plethora of subcultures from rat-rod builders to tattoo freaks and they get along well together. So much so, you might say it's a 'family' atmosphere. You can only get in with a full weekend ticket – which should deter the spectators – and a well developed campsite means your Airstream is more than welcome.

www.hotrodhayride.com
www.retrophoto.co.uk

Hollywood Cricket Club

Photography: *Matt Hind*
Text: *Howard Mutti-Mewse*

Left: C. Aubrey Smith at a fundraising match, held at Gilmore stadium, Los Angeles. Wearing Hollywood Cricket Club blazer in 1945 (Getty Images).

From waist-tied sashes of the eighteenth century to the brightly coloured blazers and distinctive ties and caps of the 1910s, cricket has long been a refuge for eccentric sporting Englishmen and colonial exiles in need of a reminder of home. It was during the Edwardian epoch that contemporary sartorial standards in formal English menswear were set and the look of cricket apparel was no different. Here we look at the efforts of veteran cricketer C. Aubrey Smith to maintain those standards in dress and decorum on the cricket pitch in the far-off land of America.

C. Aubrey Smith (1863-1948) was for much of his life an "Englishman abroad" and in 1932 started the Hollywood Cricket Club in Los Angeles, California. Matches became prominent fixtures in the weekly social diaries of the British expat. community and surprisingly the Hollywood elite. A man for whom the term "quintessentially English" could have been invented, Aubrey Smith learned to play cricket at Charterhouse School, going on to play for Cambridge University and Sussex and succeeding the great W.G. Grace as Captain of England against South Africa in 1889. He was also a regular in the Gentlemen vs. Players fixtures of the 1890s held annually at the home of the MCC, Lord's Cricket Ground.

In 1929 and by now a successful actor, Smith moved to Hollywood where, taking advantage of his height (6ft 4 inches), manner and appearance he quickly became Hollywood's favourite English gentleman-in-residence. Ignoring the fact that the sun was rapidly setting on the British Empire, this self-appointed cultural ambassador was keen to develop social ties with fellow Brits. In 1932, five cartloads of imported English grass seed were planted

to establish a permanent wicket at Griffith Park, the first home of the HCC. Like a distant uncle from a P.G. Wodehouse story we can only speculate that this site represented the eccentric actor's very own interpretation of Rupert Brooke's "Corner of a Foreign Field".

Over the years, famous members of Hollywood Cricket Club would include David Niven, Basil Rathbone, Cary Grant, Douglas Fairbanks Junior and P.G. Wodehouse. When Lawrence Olivier arrived in Hollywood in 1933 he was immediately summoned to net practice. Olivier dutifully attended in a borrowed pair of size 13 boots, lent to him by horror film star, Boris Karloff, another pillar of the "Hollywood Raj" made famous by his role as Frankenstein in 1931.

Dress code for the club was strict and Aubrey Smith used his connection with Eric Kent (founder of London based outfitters Kent and Curwen*) to secure authentic cricketing attire for his players. Hollywood Cricket Club may not have been the most devastating team ever to take to the field but with the likes of (Tasmanian native) Errol Flynn keeping wicket they were undoubtedly the most glamorous. Taking tea in the warm California sun against the magenta backdrop of the Hollywood Hills, the team must have cut a dash in their green, black and gold blazers and crisp white flannels.

From its illustrious beginnings Hollywood Cricket Club continues to play a major role in California's cricketing scene. Whilst the club is now based further west in suburban Woodley Park and the glamour of a bygone era associated with the club is gone, the spirit of C. Aubrey Smith lives on.

*Kent and Curwen were the main outfitters for the England and Australian Cricket teams until 1990s.

Links

www.kentandcurwen.co.uk
www.hollywoodcc.hitscricket.com
www.lords.org

112

Above: Mr Patrick Gillet wears original 1930s Hollywood Cricket Club blazer, courtesy of the MCC archives.

Special thanks to Adam Chadwick and the MCC for allowing *Men's File* special access to photograph their extremely rare collection of cricket caps and blazers.

113

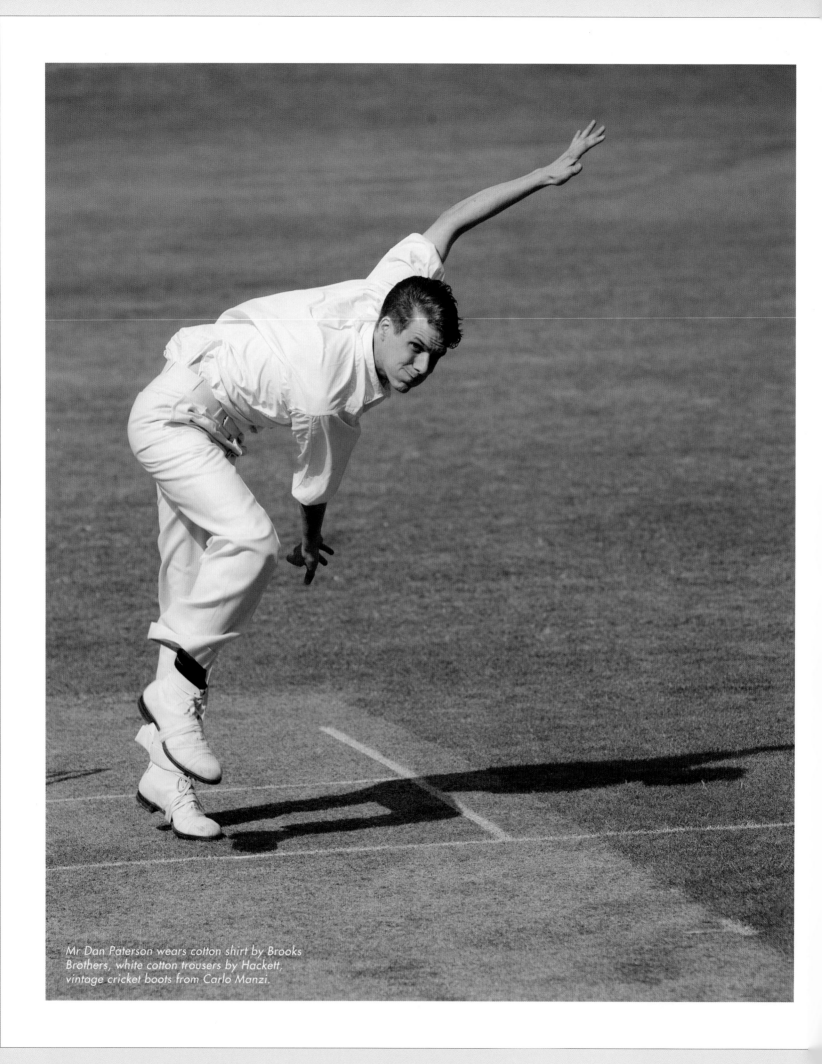

Mr Dan Paterson wears cotton shirt by Brooks Brothers, white cotton trousers by Hackett, vintage cricket boots from Carlo Manzi.

Cricket

Photography and Text: *Matt Hind*
Wardrobe: *Mitchell Belk*
Grooming: *Richard Scorer at Harringtons using L'Oreal*

Vitaï Lampada and the summer of 1980

There's a breathless hush in the Close tonight
Ten to make and the match to win
A bumping pitch and a blinding light
An hour to play and the last man in
And it's not for the sake of a ribboned coat or the selfish hope of a season's fame
But his captains hand on his shoulder smote
"Play up! Play up! And play the game!"

(Vitaï Lampada Sir Henry John Newbolt 1897)

Whilst matron was measuring my inside leg one early Summer's morning to match me up for a pair of oversized hand me down flannels, worn by one hundred boys before me, the last thing on my mind was poetry. Scraping into the Second XI had earned me the right to visit matron and her small team of highly attractive seamstresses who would pick out my kit from bowing shelves bearing the weight of 50 years worth of discarded, naphthalene infused cricket whites. Chance played its part. I knew from experience that an unfashionable selection by our school nurse could render one sartorially challenged in the outfield. On the other hand the right collar and tapered trouser might help me score a half century and look a little bit like David Bowie. Forehead itching with a slight perspiration accompanied by the merest suspicion of a facial flush as matron's tape measure brushed against my middle wicket, I contemplated being bowled first ball!

The dice was thrown and matron came up trumps (*anyone ever mention mixing metaphors? Ed.*). I felt that without having much to say in the matter the female hand of fate had made me stylish. With a double pleated trouser and one inch turn-ups, I was the Thin White Duke of Cheltenham Boy's College's Second XI.

Walking out to bat with a beloved Grey Nicholls single scoop with split rubber grip in a borrowed pair of 1950's calico ankle boots, tapered flannels and cable knit to face the advance of an anonymous fast bowler was like walking alone onto a stage, always for the first time. Important to note, the cut of one's jib always helped make the walk back slightly more bearable.

115

Vintage cricket boots from Carlo Manzi.

Mr Tim Wilds wears a vintage cricket blazer from Cassie Mercantile.

Culford school cricket pavilion.

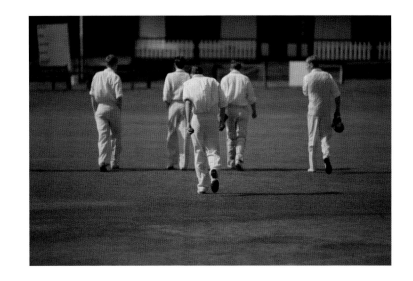

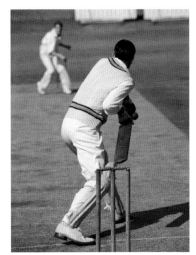

Ceremonial vintage cap, stylist's own.

Mr Tim Wilds wears a traditional wool cricket cap by New and Lingwood, shirt by New and Lingwood, sleeveless cricket jumper from Crystal Knitwear, cotton trousers by Hackett.

118

Mr Michael Doorly wears a silk neck scarf from New and Lingwood. Vintage cricket blazer from Cassie Mercantile, trousers by Hackett.

120

Tim Wilds wears a traditional wool cricket cap by New and Lingwood, shirt by New and Lingwood, sleeveless cricket jumper from Crystal Knitwear, cotton trousers by Hackett.

Our team of cricketing gentlemen wear a selection of traditional cable knit sweaters from Crystal Knitwear, Brooks Brothers and New and Lingwood. All cotton shirts supplied by menswear costumier Carlo Manzi. Cap by New and Lingwood, all trousers by Hackett.

Mr Dan Paterson wears a
cotton shirt by Thomas Pink.
Trousers by Brooks Brothers.

1. OUTSWINGER

2. INSWINGER

3. GOOGLY

4. LEG BREAK

5. OFF CUTTER

6. OFF BREAK

Mr Dan Paterson wears a traditional cashmere
cricket jumper by Kent and Curwen.

Thanks and Links:
Men's File would like to thank menswear costumier **Carlo Manzi** and **Graham Cassie**, specialist vintage
collector and shop by appointment (www.cassiemercantile.com). Traditional cable knit cricket sweaters made to
order by www.crystalknitwear.com. Traditional gentleman's outfitters – www.newandlingwood.com

Other Links
www.hackett.com
www.brooksbrothers.com
www.kentandcurwen.com

124

From Malibu to San Onofre

California Classic, the Roots of Surf Style in the Golden State

Photography and text: Gabe Sullivan

With Southern California's once emerging surf subculture now seemingly well past the point of complete saturation, it's tempting to take a nostalgic look back to those simpler one-fin times of the late 1950's and early 60's at surf Meccas such as Malibu and San Onofre.

Los Angeles-based clothing designer Kio Inagaki is especially fascinated with this time period because of its "refined style and uniqueness—a time before all the mass-production and commercialism, when surfers were riding their locally shaped boards and wearing clothes made in the USA." Inagaki's Yellow Rat label is inspired by clothing worn by early members of the WindAnSea Surf Club along with legendary surfers Phil Edwards and Lance Carson. Speaking of Edwards and Carson, their surfboards are on display at the Surfing Heritage Foundation in San Clemente—which houses over 150 surfboards and serves to illustrate the evolution of surfboard design. The collection contains Simmons, Quiggs, Kivlins, Velzys, Brewers and includes boards ridden by the likes of Gerry Lopez, Duke Kahanamoku and numerous other legends of the sport. Also on display is a shaping shack built with wood from the late Dale Velzy's old fence. It's filled with Velzy's tools and a balsa blank rough shaped by him.

Eli Viszolay wears: Replica WindAnSea Surf Club jacket by Duffer, black pocket t-shirt and Replica WindAnSea Surf Club nylon trunks by Yellow Rat, hand-woven coconut palm leaf hat by Walter Viszolay.

Linus Morris wears: Competition stripe trunks and pocket t-shirt by Yellow Rat, Wayfarer sunglasses by Ray-Ban.

Up and coming San Clemente-based shaper Donald Brink recently visited Velzy's shaping shack where he felt an "incredible appreciation for (Velzy's) dedication to custom-built wooden boards—it was so much more of a labor of love back in those days." Brink's appreciation also stems from his personal experience shaping balsa wood surf craft inspired by the finless hot curl boards from the early '50's. For his Revolver label, Brink looks at retro concepts for inspiration and builds user-friendly boards for the modern surfer. "There is definitely a trend right now where people are riding classic and retro boards without shame. You can go down to San Onofre today and watch kids drawing elegant lines with the class and style of the forefathers of surfing."

One such forefather is Walter Viszolay from Laguna Beach who started surfing in 1961, and now at 61 years old, still shapes and rides his own wooden longboards. "Being a surfer back then when not many people were doing it was really special. Things have changed now, but I still manage to find places that aren't crowded where I can enjoy surfing similar to how it was back then—with my son Eli—now." And so it goes—the spirit of surf stoke gets passed along to the next generation.—Gabe Sullivan

Production: Point & Shoot
Props: Norm Clark
Surfboards: Surfing Heritage Foundation
Vehicles: Brian Bent and Steve Stewart

surfingheritage.org
yellow-rat.com
captainfincompany.com
pointandshootproduction.com
deltabravoblog.blogspot.com

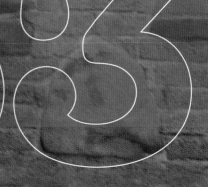

Eli Viszolay wears: Striped t-shirt by Levi's Vintage Clothing, vintage corduroy pants by Levi's.

Donald Brink wears: Competition stripe windbreaker by Yellow Rat, jeans by Levi's.

Sierra Sullivan wears: Polka dot halter bathing suit by Pret-á-SURF,
Wayfarer sunglasses by Ray-Ban.

Linus Morris wears: Checkered trunks by Standard California.
Eli Viszolay wears: 2mm short John wetsuit by Captain Fin Co.
Walter Viszolay wears: Trunks by Yellow Rat and his own hand-woven coconut palm leaf hat.

Eli Viszolay: Striped trunks by Yellow Rat.

Donald Brink wears: Vintage striped pocket t-shirt by K Mart, jeans by Levi's.
Eli Viszolay wears Plaid sport shirt by Yellow Rat.

Donald Brink wears: Pocket t-shirt and trunks by Yellow Rat.

71

Heaving Line: A Day on the Infanta

Walking into our office in Holborn this spring, Mr Duran Brown, a young actor, approached the editor's desk, threw down an ancient brown envelope and said "take a look". Sage-like and saying nothing, our Ed. opened the package and spread a group of old photographs and a printed sheet on the polished walnut surface. We could see his mind ticking over, the logistics, the clothes, the crew, – the cost. Two months later we were heading down to Cowes, the world epicentre of sports sailing.

The main inspiration for these photographs is Heaving Line – the weekly newspaper of the US Maritime Service training station at Sheepshead Bay, Brooklyn, NY. The USMS was formed in 1938 to build a more efficient and powerful merchant fleet in the United States. Highly utilised during the Second World War, several training stations opened on the East Coast and in California to support the war effort. Sheepshead Bay operated between 1942 and 1954 teaching seafaring skills such as sailing and rowing and encouraging sports like swimming and boxing.

Photography: Nick Clements

The crew: Duran Brown, Sonya Frances, Michael Doorly, Ryan Burr, Eddy Taylor. Hair and make-up: Lisa Pemberton.

Pictured right is the Cowes based, American built yacht the Infanta with our own *Men's File* crew of young sailors wearing maritime clothing with an American mid-century theme. First floated in 1947 this 47' Bermudan Yawl is the type of vessel that would have been present during the 1930s, 40s and 50s up and down the East Coast from Maine to the Carolinas.

buzzricksons.com   union6.com   thecurator.co.uk

94

classicyachtcharters.eu

Duran wears: USN denim fatigues smock by The Curator.

Eddie wears: Chambray shirt by Union 6.

Sonya draws rope from tote bag by Union 6.

Canvas duffle bag by Heritage Research, USN purse from the collection of Mr Duran Brown.

Duran wears: Chambray shirt by Buzz Rickson's, black merino wool base-layer by Endura, USN denim dress pants by The Curator.

Ryan wears: jacket and leggings by Levi's Vintage Clothing, black merino wool base-layer by Endura.

Eddie and Ryan wear: Denim fatigue pants by Levi's Vintage Clothing.

Mike wears: USN G-1 type leather jacket by Heritage Research.

Sonya wears: Chambray shirt and twill fatigue pants by Levi's Vintage Clothing (women's), black merino wool base layer by Endura.

Duran wears: Chambray shirt by Buzz Rickson's, black merino wool base-layer by Endura, USN denim dress pants by The Curator.

Duran and Mike wear: USN denim fatigue smock and dress pants by The Curator, black merino wool base-layer by Endura.
Wool watch cap by Buzz Rickson's Ryan wears: Twill chore jacket and denim fatigue pants by Levi's Vintage Clothing.

Duran wears: Daisy Mae fatigue
hat from the collection of Union 6.

Sonya wears: Chambray shirt
by Levi's Vintage Clothing (women's).

The Mountainside at Evening

Now even falls
And fresh, cold breezes blow
Adown the grey-green mountain side
Strewn with rough boulders, Soft and low
Night speaks, her tongue untied
Darkness to darkness calls

Tis now men say
From rugged piles of stones
Steal shapes and things that should be still;
Green terror ripples through our bones,
Our inmost heart-strings thrill
And yearn for careless day.

Robert Graves 1911

George Mallory (the mountaineer) was a teacher at Charterhouse School where Robert Graves (the novelist and poet) was one of his pupils. Considering the social structure of Edwardian Britain the fact that two public figures shared a public school classroom is hardly unusual. What is uncanny is – the school boy – Graves' prophetic elegy to Mallory thirteen years before his demise during a summit attempt on Everest with fellow climber Sandy Irvine.

Mallory's fully clothed body was finally discovered on the mountain in 1999 giving us insight into his preparation for the ascent. Tweed, silk and cotton were used in layers beneath a cotton gabardine shooting style jacket with underarm action-gussets for full movement. In 2006 Everest veteran Graham Hoyland spent two days on the upper slopes of Everest wearing replicas of the Mallory clothing and found it to be light and comfortable and judged it sufficient for the Edwardian climber's survival.

Inspired by this practical story and the romance of Graves' poem, *Men's File* sent photographer Matt Hind to the heart of the Tirol, on the boarder of Germany and Austria, to meet two accomplished alpine climbers for a tweed-clad attempt on the Karwendel mountain in Mittenwald. Well known to the two climbers, Bernd Schair and Iver Morrison,

these dangerous slopes presented a more than
sufficient challenge with high winds, snow drifts
and a temperature of minus eight centigrade –
during May.

Seeking shelter in a mountain hut, Hind grabs
shots seldom seen (I think NEVER seen: Ed.) within
the realm of style or fashion as the climbers
retreat from the weather and emerge through the
twilight and driving snow at over 2000m. After the
climb the trio explore the surrounding countryside
of Bavaria and visit the small towns that have
changed little since the British pioneered modern
mountaineering in the Alps in the second half of
the nineteenth century.

Photography: Matt Hind

111

Bernd wears Ventile cotton Antarctic parka and woolen naval jumper by Nigel Cabourn.

Bernd wears grey Harris Tweed Mallory jacket by Nigel Cabourn.
brown Derby boots by Trickers.
Vintage tweed plus fours by Carlo Manzi.

Bernd wears 3 piece grey Harris weed herringbone suit and navy flannel Canvey cap by Old Town.
White penny collar shirt made to order by Alexander Boyd.

Iver Morrison wears grey Harris Tweed
jacket and waistcoat by Old Town.
Vintage woolen tie by Ralph Lauren.

Bernd's Rucksack by Nigel Cabourn.

stylefile

TO TRACE THE roots of style is a clear objective but there is a route-map to such a journey. In this chapter we select five pillars of influence: military, auto-sport, music, sartorialism and the hand-made item, and American college or Ivy League dress as key themes. Central to the design of all men's apparel and associated objects, these fields of endeavour will lead us safely through the deserts of mass consumption and confused historicity.

The subculture of military re-enactment is investigated so that a human, and thus creative, dimension to historical dress can be reviewed and World War II garments pictured as they are worn today. For myself as editor this approach animates dead histories and offers inspiration to clothing makers today who might want to exploit this area of continued research. I'm sure that *Men's File* is the first style publication to see re-enactment in terms of style, but that only highlights the very closed attitude of the mainstream fashion papers. Sport, and in particular auto-sport, continues to affect modern dress in a profound way but, yet again, the great stylists cannot be ignored. Mike Hawthorn, Graham Hill, Barry Sheene, Giacomo Agostini *et al* exist in the archives as models by which many standards of elegance are set.

It is said that it was the Regency dandy George Brummell who instigated the cut of the modern suit. Since that epoch the jacket, waistcoat and trousers have been formalized into a few set styles, the creation of which has become an art form in places like Savile Row. The same can be said for hand-made shoes and here *Men's File* offers an insight into the hand-made item and those for whom such luxuries are a necessity. Minute areas from the vastness of music culture are tapped for graphics, political defiance and elegance and finally a re-enactment of fraternity house life is orchestrated to chronicle the Ivy scene as it is today. Based just on these few categories, one thousand issues of *Men's File* could have be born.

68
Images of Goodwood

The Mid-Century Re-lived in Fine English Countryside

There's no shortage of purist detractors of the Goodwood Revival for being too public, too mainstream and diluted by commercialism: but still they come.

After all, without the paying spectators the participants simply wouldn't be able to perform on such a generous stage.

It's at the Goodwood Revival, usually staged during the second weekend in September, that some of the most dislocated groups rub shoulders and ideas cross-pollinate. Where else in the world would classic Ferrarri owners, A35 tuners and ton-up boy revivalists be able to admire each other's hardware (oooh matron! – Ed.)?

WWII re-enactors set up camp on the front lawn by the entrance and cruise the grounds in period Willy's Jeeps as micro-car club members pump ancient carburettors with petrol soaked fingers. Sopwith's and Spitfires fly overhead and a Howard Hughes style Spartan Executive sits on the airfield. All this in some of the most beautiful countryside Britain has to offer.

You can see the best in aircraft, motorcycles (many British but not all), scooters, buses and coaches, heavy goods vehicles and even bicycles at Goodwood. Most are of the mid-century period and all active within the enclosed area around the circuit. Then there's the racing that continues through the entire three days, in which cars that have known the glory of wins at Le Mans, the Targa Florio or Spa thunder around the ancient track piloted

'70

by former champions, but it's the pre-1966 car park where it all happens. In a public area, for which you need no ticket, is one of the largest collections of rare and exotic cars to be found anywhere in the world. Sauntering through the thousand or so cars on casual display you see examples from the sublime to the beautifully ordinary and everything in between from a 300SL Gullwing Mercedes to a special bodied Michelotti Triumph.

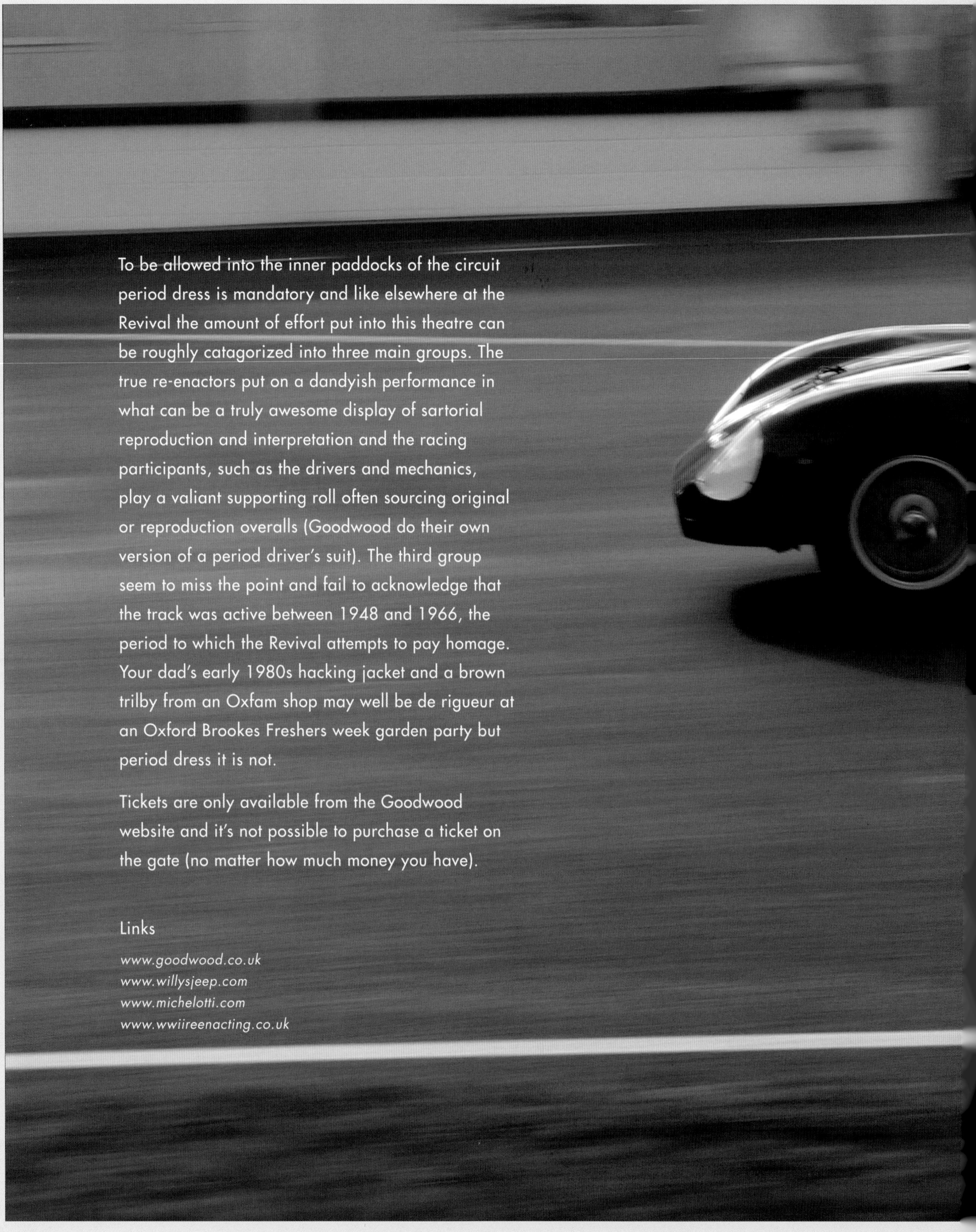

To be allowed into the inner paddocks of the circuit period dress is mandatory and like elsewhere at the Revival the amount of effort put into this theatre can be roughly catagorized into three main groups. The true re-enactors put on a dandyish performance in what can be a truly awesome display of sartorial reproduction and interpretation and the racing participants, such as the drivers and mechanics, play a valiant supporting roll often sourcing original or reproduction overalls (Goodwood do their own version of a period driver's suit). The third group seem to miss the point and fail to acknowledge that the track was active between 1948 and 1966, the period to which the Revival attempts to pay homage. Your dad's early 1980s hacking jacket and a brown trilby from an Oxfam shop may well be de rigueur at an Oxford Brookes Freshers week garden party but period dress it is not.

Tickets are only available from the Goodwood website and it's not possible to purchase a ticket on the gate (no matter how much money you have).

Links

www.goodwood.co.uk
www.willysjeep.com
www.michelotti.com
www.wwiireenacting.co.uk

Made Exclusively for *Men's File*
The ~~Lobb~~ Prospector Boot

A collaboration between
Mr. Jonathan Lobb and *Men's File*

by *Jonathan Campbell*

76

I love shoes so therefore I love Lobb. After all, they make the finest bespoke shoes in the world.

But everyone who owns a pair of these hand-stitched pieces of sartorial art owes a debt of gratitude to a modest working class boot. John Lobb was unable to break into the lucrative London Bootmaker market. So, he boarded a ship bound for the Australian gold rush to make his own fortune. Prospectors needed boots and Lobb had an idea. He created a sturdy boot with a secret compartment in the heel for prospectors to keep their precious gold nuggets. He made his fortune, returned to London and the rest, as they say, is history.

After an exhaustive search which included contacting Australian museums and the V&A who both said "good luck and let us know if you find a pair" I decided to give Lobb a call. A soft well-spoken voice answered. It was Jonathan Lobb who is the great great great grandson of the founder. We discussed the possibility of recreating the Prospector's boot. He invited me to pop down and meet him at their shop.

The Shop

On an unseasonably, beautiful sunny day in March I'm on foot negotiating the traffic accelerating outside the Lobb Shop in the middle of St James's Street.

Its façade is simple, plain, and slightly shabby but to the discerning eye it screams old money. It's in the heart of old London, from a period when St John's Wood was considered to be in the country and St James's was where the Prince Regent popped out to shop.

This was the area where Beau Brummell grew up and promenaded as the first Dandy. It's where gentleman have hung out for centuries, it caters for all their needs from shirts to cigars.

Drunk on my own romantic view of London I nearly get hit by a black cab. We exchange pleasantries in the only way Londoners know how these days. Needless to say we didn't apologise and doff hats.

As I enter a wonderful aroma of leather, wood and polish mixed with some dust fills the atmosphere. Large Victorian display cabinets line one side of the shop housing the huge variety of shoes and boots that Lobb could make for you.

There's a cabinet full of spurs and another with interesting paraphernalia like Queen Victoria's lasts. She had incredibly tiny feet. The furniture is old with a wonderful rich patina and the only thing that divides the shop or customer area from the workshop is an old threadbare carpet. If a customer sits on a certain chair for their fitting they'll get covered in the shavings from the last maker.

There's a book full of famous film stars and industrialist's feet which contains detailed drawings, not like an artist would make, but the simple lines and measurements created by artisans.

When Jonathan Lobb appears he is exactly as I imagined; thin, neat, smart and in possession of a calm and pleasant personality.

He shows me the rolled up hides of leather and where the "Clicker" cuts out the pattern and then we go into the surprisingly huge basement where there are piles of ancient documents. It is here the soles and heels are made. I poke my nose into a side room and find three shoemakers silently attaching the soles to the uppers. Each stitch takes about three minutes.

We then enter the "Raiders of the Lost Ark" storage area; Jonathan is standing amongst thousands of pairs of neatly alphabetically stacked lasts. Every customer they've ever had is in there. I marvel that this place exists at all let alone beneath one of the busiest streets in London.

I ask Jonathan about the Prospectors boot and he explains that they lost a lot of their archive when

they were bombed in the war. We discuss the idea of him recreating the boot that was the foundation of his family's business and he agrees.

Creating the boots.

After several visits and email conversations Jonathan and I decide to base the design on the classic "Navvy" boot, which is the basis of a working boot and we choose a riding boot leather called Albion Grain, which is a wonderfully textured chocolate brown. The boot will have a bellow tongue for weather protection and five eyelets and three hooks at the top of the boot.

The sole needs to be thick, as does the heel if we're going to have a secret compartment and Jonathan suggests updating the design with an internal sleeve pocket inside the boot to hide modern valuables. Because it's a working man's boot it needs a toecap but nothing fancy here, just two simple stitches over the top, no brogueing or notching. That would be too fussy.

The new boots are being made for Jonathan to wear so his last is used by Charlotte who is the pattern cutter; she skilfully cuts out the quarters then the vamp and lays them on the last, she's not just ensuring that the boots will fit perfectly but that they'll also look elegant.

Akie, who is the Japanese "clicker" cuts the leather to the templates created by Charlotte. She lays the wonderful leather from a French tannery over her work bench. As she stretches the leather, searching for any imperfections, she tells me that this leather feels special because it comes from a cow that wasn't forced to grow. Industrial farming demands cattle put weight on quickly which affects the quality of their hides. She sharpens her blade between every precise cut.

Because bespoke boots take at least three months to make you can continue reading the making of the Lobb Prospector's boot in the next edition of *Men's File*.

The Paper pattern is cut and fitted.

The selected leather is cut.

A 'clicker' at work.

A blade is sharpened.

An existing boot on which the prospector might be based.

A shoe maker waxes a thread.

Historical boots on display in the shop.

THE LOBB
PROSPECTOR BOOT

Part 2

In the first edition of *Men's File* we decided to re-create the boot that was the foundation for the Lobb family business. Lobb would go on to become the finest bespoke shoemakers in the world and the Loots, which had a secret compartment in the heel wherein prospectors could hide their gold, became an international sensation.

BY JONATHAN CAMPBELL

On my return to Lobb, Jonathan Lobb invites me into his office above the shop overlooking St James's. His office walls are covered in framed, hand written notes of thanks from famous people through the ages. Jonathan has a smile on his face as he presents me with the uppers of the Prospector Boots. He places them on his old desk and they sit there with temporary string laces holding them together. Without any heel or sole they appear lifeless and flaccid, yet even at this stage you can tell how amazing they're going to look; strong and tough the way a working man's boots should be. Despite this sturdiness, the detail in the stitching is beautiful and elegant. Under scrutiny the toe cap has the simple double stitch we had decided upon and I can see how thick it is with two layers of leather plus the Russet lining. The boots are fully lined. The inner sleeve pocket we added to the design as a modern secret compartment is elegantly stitched into the inside ankle of the boot. The "Tugs" are also in place. The language of shoemaking is wonderfully simple and descriptive. The "Tug" is the leather loop you use to tug the boot onto your foot. The "Bellows" tongue, which prevents water getting inside the boot, is so called because it looks like, yes, you get the idea.

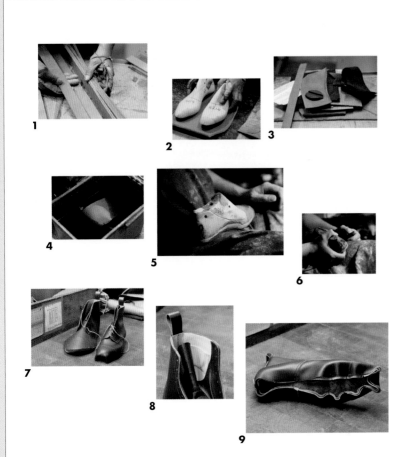

1
2
3
4
5
6
7
8
9

1 Sorting the welts
2 Lasts placed on inner sole
3 "Rough Stuff" Literally the stuff to make the boots
4 "Mellowing" Inner sole being soaked
5 "Blocking" the inner sole
6 "Shaping" wet and pliable inner sole onto last
7 Uppers
8 Close up of "Bellows" tongue, inner sleeve pocket and "Tug"
9 "Lasting over" Upper nailed to last. Two layers of leather plus Russet lining on toe.
10–14 "Lasting over"
15 Marcus makes the finest shoes in the world but doesn't wear them while he works.
16 Prepared inner sole for welt
17-18 Stitching in the wet and softened welts
19 Cutting the hole in the sole for the secret compartment
20 Offering the sole to the upper
21 Marking up the sole
22 Secret Compartment with £1 coin
23 Boots with leather laces
24 Secret Compartment
25 Nailed Heel "not neat but authentic" Hand stamped LOBB brand on sole

10
11
12
13
14

A few weeks later I'm back to watch Marcus, Lobb's master shoemaker, begin making the boots. The shoemaking happens in the basement, and as you descend the rather grand staircase you also go back in time. Surprisingly large, the basement is hot and dusty with rows of shoes waiting to be finished or polished and there's a strong smell of leather and polish that's not unpleasant. Piles of leather bound account ledgers touch the high ceiling. The huge advantage to bespoke shoes is that the customer can have pretty much whatever they want so whilst most customers opt for very traditional styles there are also those who can be extravagant. There are some beautifully made horrors down here.

Marcus, a fellow Londoner and a big man full of humour is wearing blue canvas plimsolls. He studied at Cordwainers, which is now part of The London College of Fashion, and then served his apprenticeship at Lobb under the previous master shoemaker "Ronny". Apparently, Ronny was a tough old boot but a true master craftsman and the handing down of craft skills is essential in bespoke shoemaking. Squeezing himself into the tiny workspace that he shares with two other shoemakers, Marcus estimates that it'll take three to four days to make the Prospector Boots because at 3/8ths of an inch, the soles are very thick. There's no metric system at Lobb. He also confesses to not knowing exactly how he's going to make the "Secret Compartment" in the heel, because there are no records of how John Lobb created the original boots. As he gets to work he takes a razor sharp

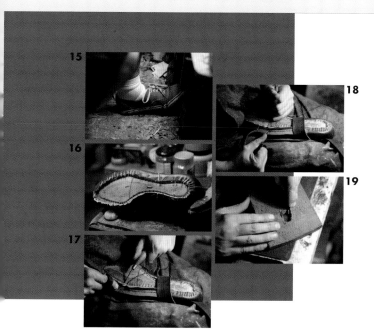

15

16

17

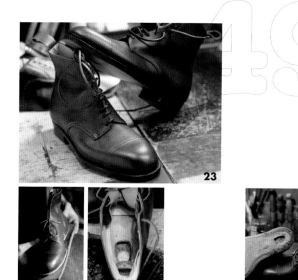

18

19

20

21   22

23

24

knife and starts to cut the straight waist of the sole. Marcus finds it amusing that we've decided to make a simple heavy working boot to show the skill of bespoke shoemakers. For him the skill in bespoke is all about creating elegant, perfectly fitting shoes. Thanks to years of experience he makes the process of shoe making look easy. Each stitch attaching the upper to the thick sole takes great skill. First he takes his spiked tool called an awl and pushes it through the hard leather, he then runs his thread skilfully over a ball made of hemp, wax and pitch, which acts as a waterproofing agent. The thread is then pushed through the hole in the sole and this laborious process goes into each and every stitch. As Marcus works meticulously and silently whilst listening to the cricket on an old transistor radio, it sounds like England could beat the Aussies. I decide to leave him in peace and on my way out I notice a cupboard adorned with a handwritten note which reads "Royal and famous lasts. Keep closed". I can't resist a cheeky peek.

A few days later, Jonathan Lobb drops me an email saying simply: "They're finished. Pop down!" So, on a warm summers day I excitedly head up to St James's and spin on my classic brown suede Gucci loafer heels into the Lobb shop, which is now so familiar to me.

Greeted by the front workshop staff (all craftsmen in their own right) I head up to the office where Jonathan, after ever so slightly wincing at my choice of shoes, places the finished boots on his desk. He then shows me how Marcus and the shoemakers created a hole in the heel which is accessed by pulling a leather flap inside the boot which is attached to a plug which fills the hole. This reveals the secret compartment, which is bigger than I expected and easily holds a £1 coin. The bottom of the heel has nails in it, which Jonathan describes as "not neat but authentic". The boots look perfect to me. Enough men bought the original boot during the Australian gold rush to make Jonathan's great, great, great Grandfather a wealthy man and gave

him the means to establish the company in London. Jonathan tells me that he's looking forward to wearing them on his scooter and that his relationship with them has only just started. Because, he reveals, the real relationship you have with your shoes isn't in the making of them but what you do whilst wearing them.

A month later my wife Majella and I are doing the dreaded back to school shoe shopping for our children. Beatrice, my five year old, demands we buy her a pair of shoes that have a secret compartment in the heel concealing a small plastic doll. Life and art move on.

www.johnlobbltd.co.uk

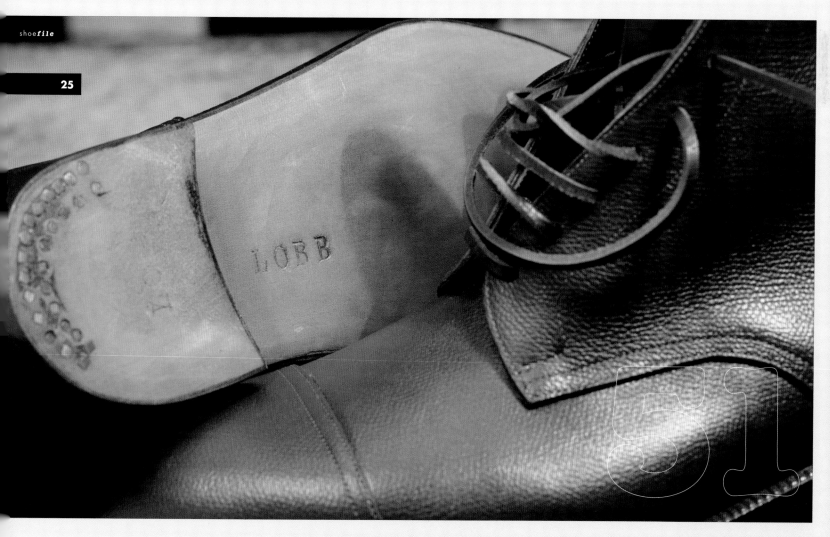

shoefile

25

LOBB

THE TRAVELLERS

Kenzaburo Ishihara (Vo. Guitar)
Shinji Takeda (T.Saxophone)
Keiji Takeda (Bass)

Photography: *Teruyuki Yoshimura*

The biggest question surrounding revival culture at all levels is: can something new form out of revival? In a mixture of homage and translation The Travellers use virtuoso musical ability to translate the sound of a traditional American jazz / blues trio of the mid-1950s. It's arguable whether or not the outcome of all creative translations results in something new and I'm not sure whether The Travellers achieve originality but they certainly pass the quality (of music) and style (in dress) exam with flying colours.

Not only does the combo hit every right note but also looks sharper than most other bands gracing any stage in any town in any country. We were not able to get an in-depth interview with the band, but from photographer Teruyuki Yoshimura's images we can scrutinise the level of dedication to detail these young gentlemen have applied to look just right. At the time of writing The Travellers are midway through a short UK tour which includes a date at the Rhythm Riot, staged mid-November at Camber Sands. If you see them and like what you see, let the organisers of the event know and maybe they'll come back next year.

www.the-travellers.com
www.rhythmriot.com

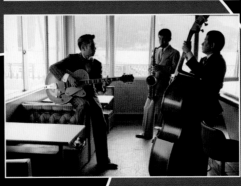

Harris Tweed
A brief history

Within the world of British textiles, the legend prevails that in 1826 a London cloth merchant took delivery of some new samples from his Scottish supplier. On the delivery note the fabrics were referred to as "Tweels", a Scottish word for a cloth with parallel, diagonal ribs (Twill) and misread by the London merchant as "Tweed". Fabric folklore or not, this generic term for carded homespun woollen fabric is now perhaps associated with the River Tweed, that would have powered most of the cloth making mills of the Scottish Borders.

When we refer to Harris Tweed a distinction must be made as it's source is far from the Boarder Country between England and Scotland and is subject to the Harris Tweed Act of 1993.

"Harris Tweed has to be woven by the islanders at their homes in the Outer Hebrides, finished in the islands of Harris, Lewis, North Uist, Benbecula, South Uist and Barra and the Outer Hebrides and made from pure virgin wool dyed and spun in the Outer Hebrides".

With a reputation for durability, tweed patterns from these islands are often characterised by the beautiful colours achieved from dyes made from lichens and heathers indigenous to the isles. For centuries inhabitants of the Western Isles have woven Clo Mhor (Gaelic for the "big cloth"). The wool for Harris Tweed is dyed. The coloured wools are then mixed together. Fibres are then teased and drawn out further by carding. The wool is then spun. All woven cloth is finished by washing and finally given a raised compact finish.

Made by hand on primitive looms until the mid 19th century all production would have been for the home. This changed in 1846 when Lady Dunmore had the Murray tartan produced in Harris Tweed. It became hugely popular as a fabric for outdoor clothing as it was ideal in the wet and windy environment of the deerstalker, salmon fisherman, ghillie and gamekeeper.

By the 1890's mainland mills as far a field

86

as Yorkshire were exploiting the demand for this highly regarded cloth using machine spun yarn and mechanised looms. Harris Tweed from the Outer Hebrides was still produced traditionally. Born out of a need to identify the Tweeds from Harris and the other Western Isles as a superior, traditionally made product, The Harris Tweed Association was set up in 1906. The Harris Tweed Authority was then established as the association's successor by The Harris Tweed Act (1993) giving the fabric statuary protection from imitation. Like a Roquefort cheese or Parma ham it is essentially copyrighted. Since 1911, each 50-yard length of fabric is inspected by The Harris Tweed Authority and hand stamped with the Orb symbol guaranteeing its provenance.

Photo: Getty Images

Master of ceremonies, Mr Johnny Vercoutre.

Fire dancer, Ms Rebecca Horrox (left) and other esteemed guests.

The White Blackbird Tweed Party
Photography: Matt Hind

It's surprising there are so few party organisers of this type. A stately location is chosen near to London but in a rural setting, a traditional theme is also selected and a dressing up box provided. This is a revival of the world of the 'bright young things' of the Edwardian epoch and the location for the White Blackbird parties matches perfectly.

This is not a re-enactment party as most people are attracted to the decadence and not the style, although there is a hardcore of style leaders including Time for Tea (Shoreditch) owner Mr Johnny Vercoutre who places some suitable 78s on the turntables, shows films and acts as ring master during the games and events that take place throughout the evening. There's also plenty of drink, good food, stores selling vintage clothing, a bit of Burlesque (although there could have been more!) and the glamorous Ms Rebecca Horrox doing a fire dance with real fire.

thewhiteblackbird.com

93

WHAT'S HAPPENING AT
TROY LEE DESIGNS
Photography and text by Gabe Sullivan

A new shop catering to Southern California's growing sector of motorcycling, surfing and skateboarding cross-cultural pollinators hosted the first annual Motorcycle Rally and Concourse de Moto in celebration of their grand opening. The steady rotation of tight rockabilly acts onstage, 'moto art show' and pin-up girl contest drew an eclectic crowd indeed. Primarily a men's moto lifestyle shop, it is part showroom for a new line of Troy Lee Designs moto-inspired sportswear, and part retail space featuring Dues Ex Machina garb from Australia and hand-crafted Stormy Monday skateboard decks. Also on offer are custom painted helmets by Troy Lee. Of note are the gleaming, mixed media McQueen signature helmet designs. "We think Steve is cool," said store co-founder Doug Bunting, a self-proclaimed "surfer who rides motorcycles". "That's why you see so much McQueen stuff in here." In fact, the shop doubles as a memorial of sorts for the late, great speed fiend with gritty, black and white photographs of McQueen at full throttle on exhibit throughout the space.

www.troyleedesigns.com

Gabe Sullivan's portraits of the visitors at the Troy Lee event give a more candid impression of the store.

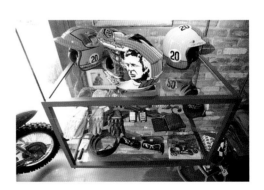

Jeep: Willys MB 1943.

Jeep Markings: Company A, 116th Infantry Regiment, 29th Infantry Division.

Eastman Leather

The other two companies featured on our makers file for issue 04 have innovative and charismatic leaders heading up a team of employees dedicated to quality and workmanship and Eastman Leather is no different. Mr Gary Eastman started collecting Second World War jackets in the 1980s and, through a mixture of curiosity and bloody-mindedness, started to mend and then remake rare and sought after models. Like so many who read and are featured in *Men's File* young Mr Eastman (he also employs his father in quality control) is a collector, enthusiast and perfectionist (if you want it right, that's a good combination! Ed).

Ever considered making a Second World War replica jacket? What about the correct zips, thread, sewing machines, leather tape and insignia? What about the finish on – let's say, a USAAF B-6? Where do you buy that particular finish of sheepskin? This is how it's done. At the workshop the unfinished, but tanned, sheepskins arrive in a pure, almost white form. The skins are laid on

a finishing table where they are carefully dyed and coated and polished and coated and coated again. Then they go through a further heat and drying process. The patterns are bought out and the skins laid on the cutting table. The specially made zips and poppers are selected and the jacket is cut and sewn. A US Army Air Force insignia is heat-sealed onto the shoulder. This is like watching a work of art being produced.

The Eastman Leather workshop is at the edge of Dartmore in an area that provided the training ground for the US Army leading up to D-Day.

Finally we should mention that Eastman also import an extensive range of Buzz Rickson's clothing as well as Lone Wolf boots and other quality accessories.

www.eastmanleather.com

35

A View of Saint James

The first impression I got when I arrived at the Normandy-based Saint James factory is one of continuity. This company has been manufacturing versions of it's own myth for over 100 years in the same way and in the same small town of St. James. No one needs to speak of the authentic at Saint James as it's implicit in the history of the place and underpinned by the fact that the classic sweaters continue to be produced no matter what the meteorological or economic climate. In a place that no one speaks of the real, the real often exists.

Started in 1850 the company originally spun yarns and then within a few years turned to producing a knitted under garment for the local fishing community as their main business. This long-bodied, long-sleeved woolen camisole (for men) went under sweaters and overalls and tucked right down below the crutch for maximum warmth. Later in the twentieth century they began to make the classic Breton style fisherman's sweater with the button fastening on the shoulder.

Entering the factory the shop floor is modern and airy. Each worker seems to have a real purpose to their activities and great care is taken over each task at hand. There are many stages in the production of a Saint James sweater from the quality control of the wool yarn as it comes into the factory to the final steam shrinking of the end garment.

Many of the knitting machines are of a traditional type and still rely on thick cast-iron or steel punch cards for their programming, giving you the feeling your sweater has been made like this for a very long time.

Interested in the styles that might have been produced in the 1950s, 60s or 70s I asked about the archive. There was bemusement, what archive? This was worrying, surely there was an archive of old styles, wider stripes and interesting colours? They said no, but I kept asking. After a lunch of local oysters and calvados we were informed that some old boxes had been pulled out of a storeroom and I could take a look. What I found inside was a treasure trove of old yellowing natural wool and blue striped garments. I need not say more as the few that are depicted on these pages tell the whole story. After this visit *Men's File* confirmed their first instinctive feelings about this company. When you wear Saint James you wear history.

www.saint-james.fr

36

Le Mont St. Michel clearly visible from the town of St. James.

Traditional knitting machines creating traditional quality.

See a small part of
the St. James archive
on the following page.

The Saint James archive: styles from the 1960s and 1970s

The original Saint James 'camisole'. Real tuck-it-in-your-pants underwear for local fishermen.

STOP PRESS! After mining the archive at Saint James, The Curator (the *Men's File* online store) will be presenting two special pre-war style VELO MOTO sweaters by Saint James. **www.thecurator.co.uk**

A Short History of Khaki

by Josh Sims

For such an inconspicuous part of the menswear wardrobe, a humble pair of khakis can fuel passions. Indeed, the collectors' market for genuine Second World War-era examples is every bit as frantic as that for vintage denim. The search, mind, is for khakis as opposed to simple chinos, the latter a generic term for any pair of sturdy cotton trousers, the former in their cut – a straight or slightly tapered leg – but especially their practical, neutral colour – a shade of putty – of military origin.

Certainly history is a large part of their appeal. It was in 1845, in India, where the story begins. In one version, soldiers first deliberately discoloured their white uniforms with not just mud but also the distinctive local dust, coffee and even curry powder in what might be considered an early stab at camouflaging – the regulation white trousers made them conspicuous targets. Indeed, khaki means dust-coloured in Urdu. In another, British Army officer Sir Harry Lumsden, commander of forces in the Punjab, sought a suitable alternative to his regulation trousers to help cope with the heat. He took to wearing lighter, looser pyjama bottoms, and had these dyed with tea leaves, later realising their benefit of camou-flage.

The route from there to the popular conception of khakis is meandering. In 1848 the British Army recognised that a colour which blended into the environment provided some military advantage was a good idea and officially adopted the shade for its colonial troops in India and for subsequent late 19th-century campaigns in South Africa, Sudan and Afghanistan. These warm weather uniforms were made in China, ostensibly to save on transport costs, and demand was such that by the 1850s the weaving of khaki fabric within the scope of the then British Empire was established; John Haller, a European weaver, introduced the first hand-looms to the Indian region of Mangalore and it is to him that the invention of khaki dye is usually attributed. As a consequence, khaki became a standard uniform colour for many armed forces.

But it was not until 1898 that the story moves to the US, khakis' spiritual home. It was during the Spanish-American War that American troops also adopted the kit and its colour for its uniforms (by a corruption of the Spanish word for Chinese comes the word chino, a word which has, of course, come to describe the more generic casual cotton trouser).

Khakis were initially adopted by the US Navy in 1912 as part of naval aviators uniform, then by submarine crews in 1931. Ten years later khakis were approved as part of senior officers' uniform during on-station duties, before these officers were finally granted permission to wear them during spells of liberty, from the end of the same year. The US version came in a lighter shade than what became known as British khaki, such that GIs referred to their khakis as suntans.

As with many garments that originated in the military but have come to have a secondary civilian life, the inspiration was partly their practicality and partly a sense of attachment among those who had had to wear them. But, above all, because the cheap, plentiful surplus stocks available at the end of hostilities found a necessary and an eager market for the cheap and hard-wearing on Civvy Street. Thus by the 1950s khakis were being worn by farm hands and college students alike.

Their appeal was further heightened by the 'man of action' image ascribed to them through their Hollywood associations, with the likes of Bogart and Cagney, Cooper and Gable all snapped in them. Khakis, as most men in the US discovered, were virtually indestructible, looked better the older they got, and as good with an Ivy League blazer as hob-nailed boots, tailoring or casualwear – all while maintaining an ageless, classless, everyman quality that first appealed to the Beat generation and still has its draw today.

There was, and is, also something of the blank canvas about them: if jeans, however varied in their detail, are redolent of workwear and westerns, always suggestive of rebellion, khakis can be worn to tinker with engines but also smartened up to parade ground standards, as their military origins required. Jeans may be tougher, more macho, but khakis are just too laid back to care. And it doesn't get cooler than that.

Khaki canvas duffle by British Khaki.

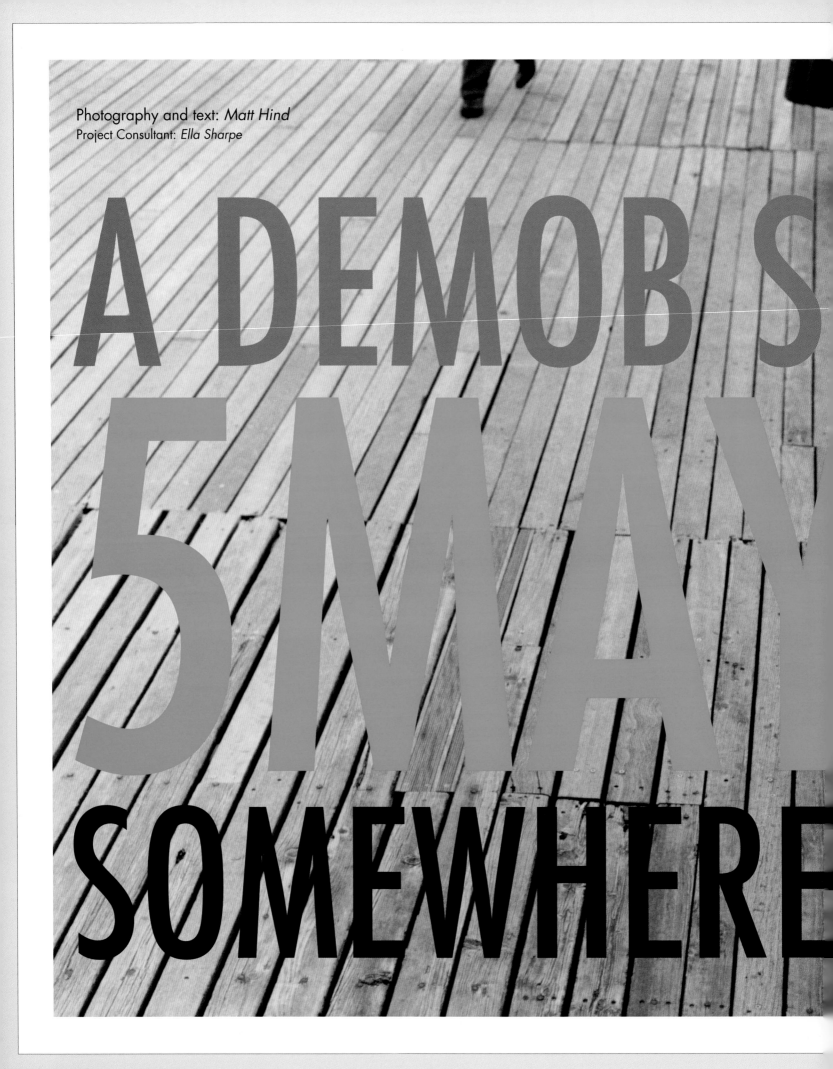

Photography and text: *Matt Hind*
Project Consultant: *Ella Sharpe*

A DEMOB'S
5 MAY
SOMEWHERE

JIT, SPRING
1,1946
IN ENGLAND

Mr Simon Delaney wears his own woollen CC41 suit and original 1940s Trilby hat.

Mr Phil Kedzle wears black leather brogues by [...].

Almost immediately after VE Day a process of demobilisation was implemented whereby 4.3 million men and women were returned to civilian life over a period of 18 months. The plan was implemented by the Minister for Labour and National Service, Ernest Bevin. A demobbed soldier remained officially a reservist and would keep the main elements of his uniform. He would be kitted out with a three-piece suit, a hat, two shirts, a tie, two pairs of socks, a pair of shoes, an overcoat and a suitcase. Despite the vast numbers of servicemen de-mobbed immediately after the Second World War, sourcing original examples of demob suits is difficult. Many people associated their demob issue with the continued period of shortages and rationing after the war and were not keen to hold onto it as things improved.

Men's File asked Ella Sharp, designer and lecturer at Coventry University's Fashion Department to research and recreate a demob suit for issue 04 Style File. Ella was given access to three demob suits held at the Leeds Museum Discovery Centre, one of which was identified as a Burton suit.

As well as producing a huge quantity of uniforms during the war Burton are credited with supplying up to a quarter of all demob suits. In her research Ella observed that despite a reputation for being poorly made the suits she referenced were well tailored with a surprising amount of hand finishing for a mass-produced garment. Here we feature the results of Ella's research. While the weight of the cloth was compromised to allow for a period colour, the results clearly illustrate that sartorial standards were maintained even during the austerity of the immediate post-war period.

Mr Phil Kedzle and companion Miss Nicola Cowee set out for a trip to the Norfolk coast from the village of Heydon in their Morris Eight Series E. Heydon is an estate-owned village in the centre of Norfolk. Undeveloped for generations, the village green is surrounded by buildings dating from the sixteenth century. The church walls renovated in the 1970s revealed some extraordinary wall paintings from the fourteenth century, dedicated to John the Baptist.

The couple meet their train and travel along the North Norfolk Railway, now a volunteer run heritage railway, also known as The Poppy Line that operates between the Georgian Norfolk town of Holt and seaside town of Sheringham. At the end of September each year the railway hosts a 1940s re-enactment weekend.

Our story ends with a promenade along the pier. Designed by architects Douglas and Arnott, the construction of Cromer's third pier was completed in 1901. In 1908 a maple-floored pavilion was added to accommodate the increasingly popular pastime of roller-skating.

www.todotrajeado.blogspot.com

Mr James Delaney returns home in the uniform of The Royal Signals.

Mr Kedzle steps out in a dark blue pinstripe demob suit, recreated by Miss Ella Sharp.

Miss Nicola Cowee wears her own 1940s vintage bird's eye [...] suit.

1938 Morris Eight Series E.

1940s style shirt by Darcy Clothing.

Mr Phil Kedzie wears recreated demob suit and carries original demob issue coat and suitcase.

93

What is Northern Soul?
A Personal Journey into Subculture

This has to come from a personal viewpoint as real objectivity concerning subculture is always problematic. Its about the journey, but where to start? Anyone know where Redruth is? Don't worry, no one knows or cares. It's a small town located in, what used to be, industrial Cornwall in the west of England and it's a place you pass between Padstow and St Ives. So what, you ask? I promise that all shall become clear in the fullness of time.

Northern Soul is a dance and music based subculture that flourished in the northwest of England at the end of the 1960s and into the 1970s. According to Northern Soul authority Niel Rushton the term was originally coined by London based journalist and record store owner Dave Godin and was aimed at matching a certain type of rare soul record with very particular customers from the north of England. It would be hard to define the exact style of (Black) music that makes up the majority of the Northern Soul catalogue in just a few words. What I can say is that it's not really like anything the wider public might understand as Soul music (although it is clearly soulful). The few records that ever touched the mainstream were R. Dean Taylor's, *There's a Ghost in my House* (UK, 1974), The Tams', *Hey Girl Don't Bother Me* (UK, 1971) and Dobie Gray's

Out on the Floor (UK, 1975). If you know those discs you might understand what I'm talking about.

My first experience of Northern Soul happened one night at a local Redruth night-spot known as the Penventon Hotel in 1975 and after that I was hooked for about eighteen months. Looking at a motorway map of Britain it seems that this dance based subculture travelled down the west of the country starting at the Twisted Wheel in Manchester, on to the Wigan Casino, down the M6 to The Torch at Stock-on-Trent then stopping-off at Wolverhampton. Moving from club to club it continued down the M5 to Bristol and finally to the end of the M5 and along the A30, ending-up at the Penventon Hotel, Redruth. That's where I was.

There were just two or three local lads who went up to Bristol and even Manchester to the mystical all-nighters and always carried with them pvc over-night bags covered in patches and stickers from such events. The younger boys, we were about fifteen, didn't dare speak to them or ask questions. We just snatched glimpses in a dark and smokey room and hoped to learn something. The DJ had about ten mainstream Northern records like *Needle in a Haystack* by the Velvelettes and novelty tracks like *Nobody But Me* by

the Human Beinz. These were played in a twenty minute Northern Soul section along with *(I get my kicks) out on the floor* (usually played two or three times) and the aforementioned R. Dean Taylor was also a weekly fixture. I waited all evening for the DJs set to start with the opening 'fog horn' intro to *Nobody But Me* and stepped onto the floor to start my own dance routine and pull as many advanced moves as possible. Timing is important as Northern records are all about reaching peaks or musical climaxes and you have to time your high-kicks or back drop to coincide with the very top of the crescendo. I also learned that perfecting the basic moves and performing them in an elegant way was actually better than attempting crazy acrobatics and doing them badly. That stood me in good stead for the rest of my life. At the start of 1977 I heard the Clash for the first time and dancing was all over for me, although I took some of the style with me into New Wave and on to Mod revival.

When I saw a stylish gentleman, of a certain age, at a recent vintage festival carrying his own original over-night bag I asked if I could photograph it for *Men's File*. This bag tells such a story.

Based on an Austin A40, The Nash Metropolitan was was made in the UK for the American export market from 1954 - 1962.

Frat House

Photography: *Nick Clements*

Started in 1953 the Ivy League is an inter-university sports association that continues to exist today between eight of America's elite Eastern colleges. It is both the standard and slightly eccentric wear of the stu-dents of Brown, Columbia, Cornell, Dartmouth, Harvard, Pennsylvania, Princeton and Yale during a decade long era, starting in the late 1950s, that has become known as the Ivy look. *(continued page 108)*

style*file*

From left to right: Cardigan by Folk,
Cardigan by YMC, Sweater by Baracuta.

101

Complete outfit by Ralph Lauren.

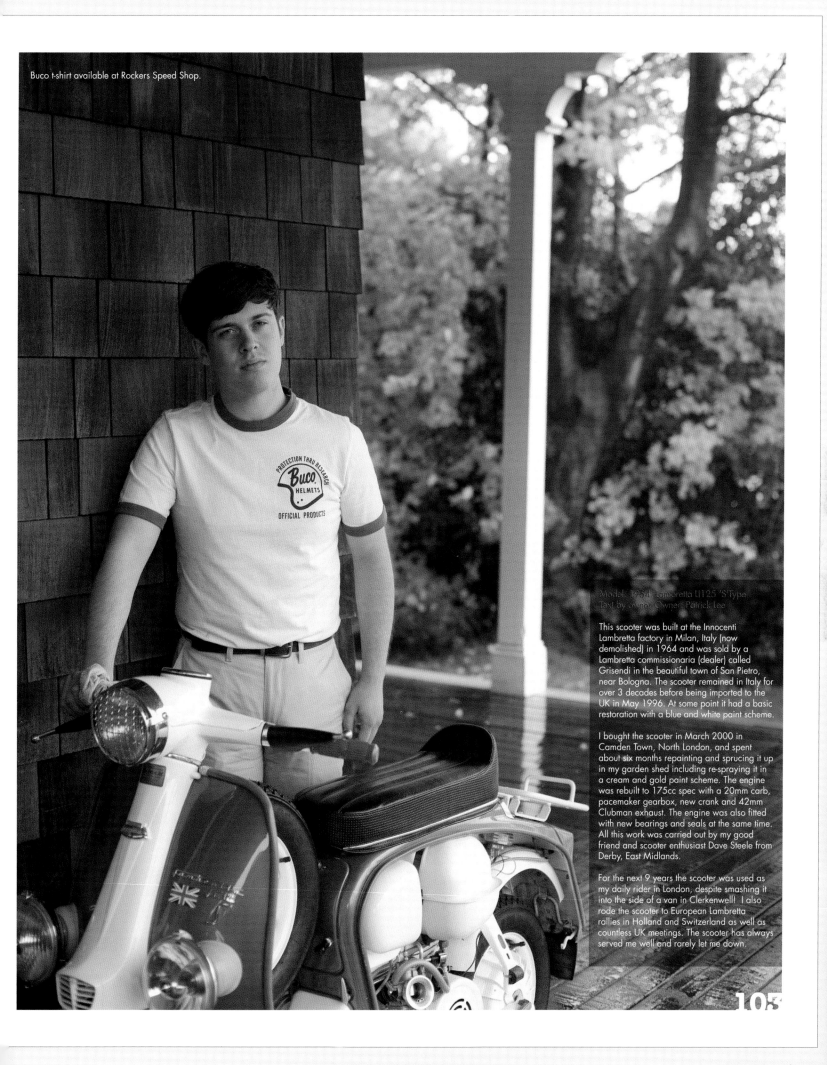

Buco t-shirt available at Rockers Speed Shop.

Model: 1964 Lambretta LI125 'S' Type
Text by owner. Owner: Patrick Lee

This scooter was built at the Innocenti Lambretta factory in Milan, Italy (now demolished) in 1964 and was sold by a Lambretta commissionaria (dealer) called Grisendi in the beautiful town of San Pietro, near Bologna. The scooter remained in Italy for over 3 decades before being imported to the UK in May 1996. At some point it had a basic restoration with a blue and white paint scheme.

I bought the scooter in March 2000 in Camden Town, North London, and spent about six months repainting and sprucing it up in my garden shed including re-spraying it in a cream and gold paint scheme. The engine was rebuilt to 175cc spec with a 20mm carb, pacemaker gearbox, new crank and 42mm Clubman exhaust. The engine was also fitted with new bearings and seals at the same time. All this work was carried out by my good friend and scooter enthusiast Dave Steele from Derby, East Midlands.

For the next 9 years the scooter was used as my daily rider in London, despite smashing it into the side of a van in Clerkenwell! I also rode the scooter to European Lambretta rallies in Holland and Switzerland as well as countless UK meetings. The scooter has always served me well and rarely let me down.

103

Cardigan, sweater and scarf all by YMC.

was now worn by young Soho jazz musicians like Zoot Money and R and B (the original kind) performers such as Georgie Fame. Fame's album *Rhythm And Blues At The Flamingo* (1964) depicts the performer at the Hammond Organ in button-down collar shirt, narrow tie and (most important) madras check jacket. It's impossible to say who was the fist to bring Ivy over the Atlantic but it was as early as 1963 that the Rolling Stones went to New York for the first time and returned head to toe in Ivy. *The Rolling Stones No.2* (1964) and the picture cover EP *Five By Five* (1964) show the band as if posing for some kind of ultra-liberal-long-hair Brooks Brothers catalogue. We can speculate that The Stones didn't see the ironic nature of the oppressed black musician wearing the clothes of the Harvard graduate or that they got it and wanted in. We will never know. What we can see in hindsight is The Stones were as much proto-Mods as Georgie Fame – often cited as being a strong influence on Mod style.

If that little history takes us to 1964, where are we today? Those who loved Ivy in the 1960s never really went away and there was at least one outlet dedicated to the style. Veteran London retailer John Simons opened the Ivy Store in Richmond in 1964, which lasted into the late 1970s, followed by J. Simons in London's Covent Garden, which recently closed down.

In America the Ivy League look became College and Preppy style. It never really went away and can still be seen in the mid-town Madison Ave. store like Brooks Brothers, J. Press, JoS. A. Bank and the shoe store Alden. It's worth mentioning that J. Press, although not well known in Europe, has been the main outfitter to the Ivy League colleges since it started in New Haven in 1902. Since the late

1970s the American College image has been appropriated and further developed by the master of American simplicity Mr Ralph Lauren who through inspired photography and a high quality workmanship has reclaimed the golden era of Ivy style for new generations (hang on – do you work for this company? Ed). RL laid down new foundations in which others have constructed variations on the theme. Hilfiger in the 1990s and then a small but highly influential design house Thom Browne have made their mark and Brown's line for Brooks Brothers called Black Fleece magnifies the style in an elegant and credible fashion.

The ultimate reference point for today's Ivy style comes, perhaps, not from an original movie or publication (although T. Hayashida's, historical Take Ivy – now available in English – is invaluable) but from a revival work by John Landis called Animal House (1978). This film crammed every Ivy look cliché into a couple of hours and was adapted from an original work for National Lampoon magazine by Chris Miller, himself a Dartmouth graduate. The architecture, cars and dress were well observed but it was also the friction caused between the two fraternity houses representing 'old order' (conservative) and 'new order' (liberal) values and latter's relationship with Black culture that made the film far more than simply stylish and hilarious entertainment.

So here we are at a fraternity house somewhere East at an unspecified college in a year we are not sure of. Dad (an alumnus) brings son and some college friends back to the chapter house. This is pure Ivy.

Stop press J. Simons should re-open at 46 Chiltern Street, London W1. **www.johnsimons.co.uk**

(continued from page 100)
In certain ways similar to foppish (British) Oxford and Cambridge style this very American aesthetic was interpreted as being emblematic of the dominant culture of the era, representing the patrition/officer class and being separate to that of the lower orders. Polished shoes, madras check sports coat, Oxford-cotton button-down collar and club tie became almost a caricature – albeit a stylish one – of privileged white youth and as such left itself wide open to be parodied and re-interpreted as a symbol of subversion.

This sartorial 'kick' happened first among the more radical (mainly black) bebop musicians, especially on the West Coast scene, but also transferred to London and Paris via the most effective visual (style) medium of the early 1960s: that of the album cover. The cover of *Workin' With The Miles Davis Quintet* (released 1959) shows Mr

Davis in a down at heel, perhaps semi-industrial area, looking like a cool college under-graduate. Giving us more clues to his agenda, his previous album *Relaxin' With The Miles Davis Quintet* (released 1958) features an illustration in the cubist style evoking the modern period. Jazz was certainly part of the modernist project, a point that would become a theme for British youth along with the 'masters' clothing that had been subversively appropriated by the 'slave' (in the form of the jazz musician).
Are you with me here?

The connection is becoming clearer, we are getting nearer to the look that would be handed back to white youth, but this time not of the leafy, gated communities of New Haven or Princeton but British youth from the clubs of Soho and the streets of West London. While still entrenched in the US as the dress of the educated establishment, Ivy

Left: his and hers duffle coats by Gloverall. This page: raincoat by Esemplare, tab collar shirt by Alexander Boyd, v-neck pullover by J.Crew, trousers by Baracuta, shoes by Bass.

109

We Made A Sharp Left Turn

Photography by: Nick Clements

Yes, we are somewhere near a Ghost Town but not in the Las Vagas Zombie way. This is the Hot Rod Church Sunday picnic blown by a brace of superchargers at the Ghost Town Road dry lake, just outside the small desert town where the Dry Lake King started his mind-bending odyssey. A jalopy club outing extraordinaire, they race and turn on the fine dust that once felt the footsteps of dinasaurs and now feels the bite of ancient cross-ply tires. At present there are more visual threads coming out of Southern California than any other place on earth and the Hot Rod Church are weaving more than their fair share.

www.hotrodchurch.com

60

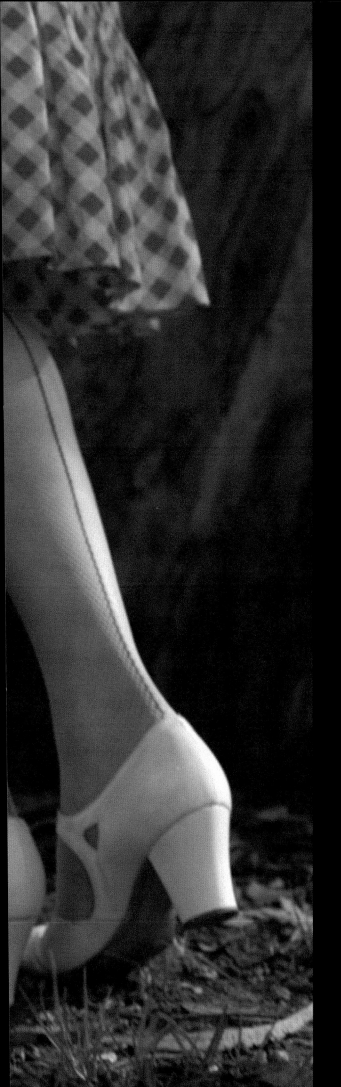

velofile

There is an internationalist dimension to *Men's File* but we are a London paper and see London things every day. Forgive me if I give a false impression – because I don't believe I do, but I have never seen, in any other world-city, so many bicycles that have been built from high quality lightweight frames and have been constructed in such a functional and elegant way. Beautiful girls ride on ancient British lightweights with hand-engraved French handlebars in this town.

Frankly, there are only a few individuals at events like the Tweed Run who can match the best of the unknowns on London streets – for the combination of machine and style – but at the Tweed Run they all come together at the same time and the effect is spectacular. Cycling, like surfing, mixes elegance, skill and endurance. This combination offers the participants the opportunity to re-enact great moments from an imagined cycling history while testing their mettle against friction and gravity. For us here at *Men's File* the most perfect place in the world to achieve such a harmonious balance is on the white roads (made from chalk) that snake through the hills of Chianti and we were there from the early days recording the Eroica bicycle rally.

L'Eroica can be a leisurely run over 38kms or so or a gruelling 205kms. You can do it in style and hardly break sweat or grit your teeth and create a very personal event that exists just between you and the cycle you probably built yourself. *Men's File* is interested in all of these so long as the machine and approach are compatible with the interests of the revival stylist who seeks information and inspiration. Standing head and shoulders above many with pretensions to cycle-style is Mr. Cally Collomon. Typical of the type of person from whom we all can learn, this man is both arch stylist and rugged participant and the feature seen in these pages is emblematic of the *Men's File* project.

L'Eroica

This event is about food, wine and up to 205km of pain. We're not talking Alpe d'Heuz but we are talking 3 to 4 mile climbs, sometimes of a slightly steep (some might call vertical) nature.

If you are into 'real' Italy then Gaiole, the village at the start and finish line, is certainly one of the epicentres. Family run osterie provide newly found white truffles with every dish and a one-man pizzeria introduces the unsuspecting customer to crusts so thin you could slip a Margherita between latch and frame and open a Yale lock.

Coincidently the owner of one of the featured workshops in this issue of Men's *File*, Lance McCormack has participated in this pageant of vintage cycling that demands high levels of fitness and bike handling skills. Set on the Tuscan countryside the event maps its route via the ancient 'white roads' of the region at four challenging levels (205km, 135km, 75km and 40km). Feeding stations on the ride look more like a five star buffet than athletic training fare and include Tuscan salumi (a selection of cold meats), crostini and Chianti wine (yes, wine).

The idea of L'Eroica (meaning: The Heroic Ones) is to offer modern folk the chance to experience the trials and tribulations encountered by the ancient racers of the heroic epoch of Italian cycle sport. Participants enter period bicycles, manufactured before 1987, wearing clothing that matches the era of the cycle. This is not a purist re-enactment but a mixture of real velo-thusiasts, club riders from around the world who want to bring back some romance to their cycling experience and a few arbiters of vintage style who see travel by bicycle as another way to express their partial disdain for mainstream life. It's a shame for these groups that a significant amount of starters do not take part in the spirit of the event and enter modern machines wearing standard spandex jerseys. (*Just ignore them: Ed.*).

Normally held on the first weekend of October you can fly to Pisa, rent a car and drive to Gaiole in about one and a half hours. It's vital to book a hotel in advance and we would recommend not leaving your travel plans to the last minute. Fag packet plans might mean getting a hotel a few miles from the start leading to a 5 mile ride at 5am at minus 5 degrees centigrade (for the longer route starters). There is no parking in or near to the village and although very cold in the morning the weather can get hot during the day. McCormack says taking part is addictive but suggests you train well before attempting it.

www.eroica.it

53

Over the L'Eroica weekend, Gaiole Village Hall hosts a really exceptional cycle-jumble.

Tweed Run

Photography: Matt Hind

Conceived by elegant graphic designer Ted Young-Ing and on its second year, this twelve mile meander through the Capital starts at the parade ground, just in front of the new Chelsea School of Art and opposite Tate Britain, and halts at the Bathhouse in Bishopsgate. There's a prize for good manners, sartorial dress and special facial hair from supportive sponsors and Bobbin Cycles provide refreshments in the form of tea and sandwiches for the poor, shattered cyclists. So what's it all about? I think you might get a clue from the route, Pimlico to Spitalfields? At the core of this event are a group of quite serious urban (Chelsea to Shoreditch) cyclists, who also hanker after the golden era of tweeds and the age of the chain. Surrounding them are less and less serious people forming concentric circles that offer less and less commitment to the cause. There are advertising executives, on fixed gear bicycles, pretending to be couriers (shame the couriers can't pretend to be executives, but they're not allowed in the building), Hoxton types with interesting facial hair (is that just for the prize? Ed.), good-looking girls and the rest. This is what one might expect from such a public event, the question is; how can the Tweed Run increase the number of real tweed cycling fanatics and reduce the regiment of extras who follow on? That will be for them to decide and us to experience next year.

tweedrun.com

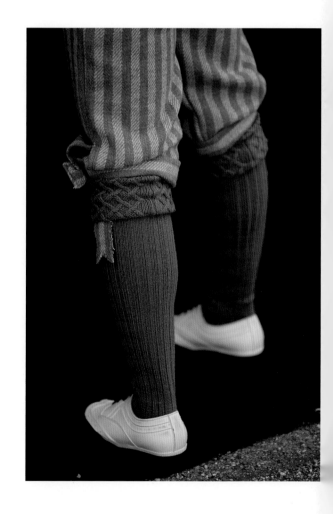

The elegant Mr. Ted Young-Ing

TWEED RUN
91

French "Constructeurs" and English Lightweights.

Photography: Matt Hind

Styling: Richard Pierce

Hair and Make-up: Fiona Moore using Dior Homme Dermo

Bicycles and accessories co-ordinated and supplied by theoldbicycleshowroom.co.uk

Hannah our cycling heroine rides through the country lanes of Norfolk on a rare Rene Herse ladies mixte bicycle. Rene Herse's machines are renowned for their build quality and comfort and the company had many successes in the "Randonneur" or amateur category of the Paris-Brest-Paris race, a gruelling 1200 km across France. Made in Paris in 1947 and sourced by vintage bike collector and enthusiast Tim Dawson for his wife, this example of the marque is in near perfect condition with original finish and lining and unusual gothic Herse script on downtube. Recognisable by the trademark duplex stem the bike has its original Rene Herse chainset. Billy accompanies Hannah riding a wonderful 650B (indicates the tyre diameter most popular in France, also known as the 26 x 1 1/2) touring bicycle by the highly reputed "constructeur " Alex Singer.

Left Men's Bicycle: Alex Singer
Right Women's Bicycle: Rene Herse
Billy and Hannah wear outfits from Cenci

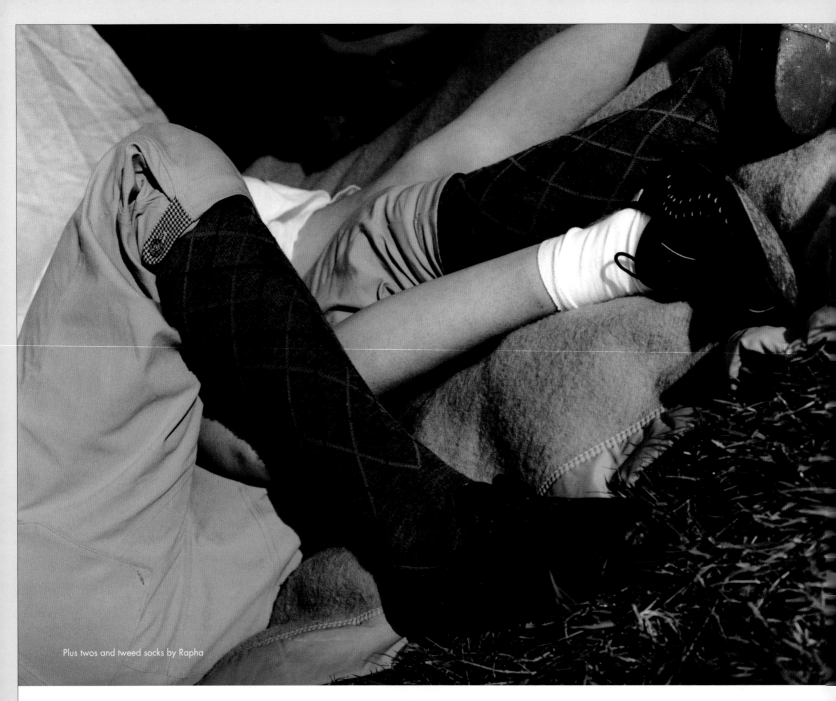

Plus twos and tweed socks by Rapha

Front pannier by
Gilles Berthoud.

Merino wool cycling jersey
by Vintage Velos.

Henry time trials an original
Paris Galibier Lightweight.
This eye-catching design was
introduced by established bike
manufacturer Harry Rensch in
1946. The company was based
in Stoke Newington, London.

It is thought the "Paris" name
was adopted during the war
to detract from the German
sounding Rensch.
An exact replica of this frame
can be purchased through
Condor Cycles.

Black merino wool polo shirt by Rapha.
Tan leather bicycle shoes by Quoc Pham.

Lightweight waxed cotton
jacket by Albam

vintagevelos.com

theoldbicycle.co.uk

vintagebicycle.wordpress.com

classiclightweights.co.uk

classicrendezvous.com

condorcycles.com

quocpham.com

velo-retro.com

hetchins.org

cenci.co.uk

rapha.cc

Billy joins Henry on a Carlton Flyer. Carlton bikes were hand-built but affordable machines, mass produced by the standards of the day but respected nonetheless by serious riders.

Collomon Goes Forth

Photography: *Matt Hind*

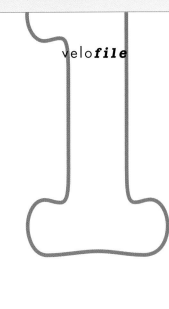

Cally Collomon, "part-time" art director, cycling historian and collector of bikes, set out on August 18th 2010 from Land's End in Cornwall, to travel the entire length of Great Britain to John O'Groats in Scotland. An 1885 Grafton Silent Compound Roadster with a 50-inch fixed wheel was his chosen mode of transport.

The generic name for a cycle of this early simple design where the pedals drive the front wheel directly is an Ordinary. They are more universally referred to today as Pennyfarthings, a reference to the difference in size between the front and rear wheels.

Along with a very modest and ad hoc support crew (a man and a van) Cally was joined by friend and member

'72

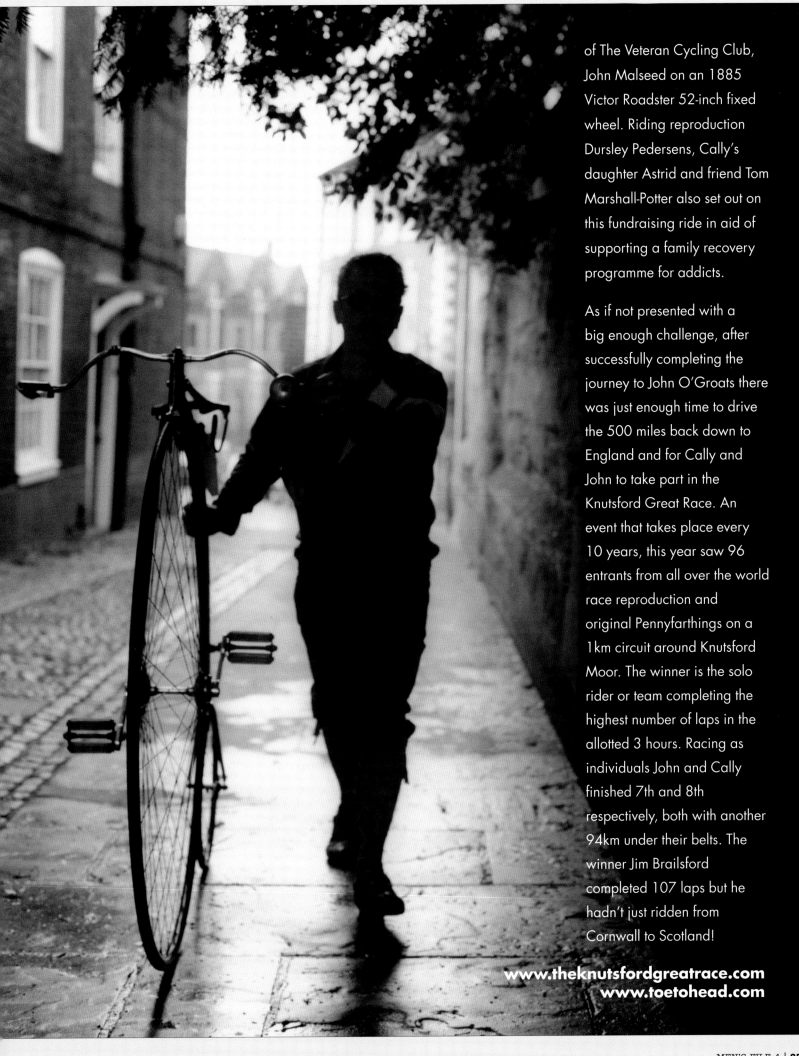

of The Veteran Cycling Club, John Malseed on an 1885 Victor Roadster 52-inch fixed wheel. Riding reproduction Dursley Pedersens, Cally's daughter Astrid and friend Tom Marshall-Potter also set out on this fundraising ride in aid of supporting a family recovery programme for addicts.

As if not presented with a big enough challenge, after successfully completing the journey to John O'Groats there was just enough time to drive the 500 miles back down to England and for Cally and John to take part in the Knutsford Great Race. An event that takes place every 10 years, this year saw 96 entrants from all over the world race reproduction and original Pennyfarthings on a 1km circuit around Knutsford Moor. The winner is the solo rider or team completing the highest number of laps in the allotted 3 hours. Racing as individuals John and Cally finished 7th and 8th respectively, both with another 94km under their belts. The winner Jim Brailsford completed 107 laps but he hadn't just ridden from Cornwall to Scotland!

**www.theknutsfordgreatrace.com
www.toetohead.com**

Appendix

Men's File Issue Listing

Photography: Neal Reed

Acknowledgements

IT'S A TIRED old phrase but totally appropriate in this case. *Men's File* has been a labour of love for all concerned and has acted as a portfolio, not only for the photographers but also for the participants who have been able to showcase their restaurants, events, architecture or collections of motorcycles, cars, clothing etc. If you are not part of the mainstream hot rod car or bike scene, a London fashionista or part of the official retro-surf scene in the bottom tip of Orange County, it's unlikely you will find a medium through which you can display your own individual labour of love. In a series of collaborations between photographers, illustrators and participants, *Men's File* moved forward. Each new issue being a six month journey into the unknown, eventually emerging as a celebration of mid-century style and the individuals who not only keep it alive but actually reshape it. The follow is a thanks to the participants:

Martin, Debbie, Wesley and Diane, Mark Upham, Ruby's Diner, All at Viva Las Vegas, Ben Cox, Daniela G., Duran Fulton Brown, Billy Price, Rebecca Horrox, Sean and Sue Peschiera, Steven Phillipson, Abbey Klee, The Fox Family, The Cycle Zombies, Jamie and Lenny, Jean-Claude Barrois, Simon Delaney, Vincent Prat, Simon Summers, Ryan Morris, George Miller, Brian Bent, David Nolan, Lance McCormack, Mark Powell, Ashley Lloyd-Jennings, Conrad Leach, Christophe Loiron, Rob Machado, Dave Hackett, Brad Bowman, Steve Olson, Lance Mountain, All at the Hot Rod Hayride, Sierra O'Sullivan, Sonia, Berndt Schair and Iver Morrison, Jonathan Lobb, The Travellers, Johnny Vercoutre, Troy Lee and Friends, Gary Eastman, Saint James, Nigel Cabourn and Drew Holmes, Phil Kedzle and Nichola Cowee, Paul and Amber, All at L'Eroica, Andy and Pandora, Ted Young-Ing And All at the Tweed Run, Richard Pierce, Cally Colloman and Hannah Regal.

Photography: Neal Reed